HEALTHY FOODS

for

HEALTHY KIDS

120 Simple, Nourishing, Gluten- and Dairy-Free Recipes Your Whole Family Will Love

PETE EVANS

Skyhorse Publishing books may be purchased in bulk at special discounts for sales promotion, corporate gifts, fund-raising, or educational purposes. Special editions can also be created to specifications. For details, contact the Special Sales Department, Skyhorse Publishing, 307 West 36th Street, 11th Floor, New York, NY 10018 or info@skyhorsepublishing.com.

Skyhorse® and Skyhorse Publishing® are registered trademarks of Skyhorse Publishing, Inc.®, a Delaware corporation.

Visit our website at www.skyhorsepublishing.com.

Please follow our publisher Tony Lyons on Instagram @tonylyonsisuncertain.

10 9 8 7 6 5 4 3 2 1

Library of Congress Control Number: 2024945734

Food photography by William Meppem, Mark Roper, Steve Brown, and Anson Smart
Food styling by Lucy Tweed, Deborah Kaloper, and David Morgan

Cover design by Kai Texel

Print ISBN: 978–1–64821–087-7
Ebook ISBN: 978–1–64821–088-4

Printed in China

This book is dedicated to all the children, moms, dads, grandparents, aunties, uncles, sisters, brothers, guardians, schoolteachers, childcare workers, hospital staff, and health-care practitioners who have the courage to step outside what is considered "normal" in our society and reclaim their health and the health of those they care most about. There is a health revolution dawning, and you are all creating the ripples that will transform and inspire others to do the same.

Love always,
Pete xo

Contents

Foreword

"Let food be thy medicine and medicine be thy food." This oft-quoted phase spoken by Hippocrates around 400 BC has never been more relevant. The prevalence of chronic illness in children has skyrocketed with an increasing reliance on prescription drugs to treat any ailment. While many factors have likely contributed to the pandemic of chronic illness in children, the addiction to processed foods, especially "fast foods," is probably a contributor. From an early age children become addicted to high-carbohydrate processed foods "contaminated" with all kinds of chemical additives. It is time that we return to a simpler age and feed our children real, wholesome, and unprocessed food. This is critical to ensure their health and vitality as well as their physical, emotional, and intellectual development. In his unique way Pete Evans provides *Healthy Foods for Healthy Kids.* The recipes are easy to follow, and the meals are simple and wholesome. Pete provides recipes for babies; this is important for parents as this helps establish healthy eating habits early in the child's life. The book is well laid out and beautifully illustrated. *Healthy Foods for Healthy Kids* should be on the kitchen shelf in every household.

—Paul E. Marik, MD

Introduction

I've spent the last twenty-plus years writing cookbooks predominantly for adults, yet my real passion lies in creating delicious, nutritious food for our growing little ones. I wholeheartedly believe that nurturing our children must be one of our absolute top priorities in life, so I felt compelled to produce a book that provided solid, up-to-date information accompanied by delicious, nutrient-dense, kiddie-friendly recipes.

While it's no secret that good nutrition needs to be established before the baby is conceived, this fact seems to have been forgotten by many. Like everything in life, prevention is key, and with the alarming rise of chronic health conditions in children, I feel it's imperative that we embrace "food as medicine" and take back what's rightfully ours . . . *optimum health*!

It's so exciting for me to think of children being introduced to a whole new world of foods when they begin a nutrient-dense diet, but I fully understand that it can feel somewhat foreign at first.

However, some good ol' patience and gentle persistence is the key to overcoming any initial resistance.

In my experience, it's easier to begin the transition with foods that are familiar—even if that means serving the same basic menu for a while and then gradually introducing new recipes and flavors.

I'm also a big believer in allowing your kids to join in and help you in the kitchen, whether it's cracking a few eggs, picking leaves off herbs, or combining a mixture. The sense of achievement that they feel from assisting you to create a meal is truly worthwhile—plus they're much more inclined to eat something that they've helped to prepare.

The best thing you can do to help with time management as a parent or carer is to dedicate one effective hour or two per week in the kitchen. It ultimately saves time, money, and resources. This time will set you up for great meals with little preparation. It means there are always fermented vegetables in the fridge, as well as beautiful dishes and nourishing broth on hand.

Every week, feel free to mix things up. Find a few recipes that are appropriate for your child's age and the time.

REGARDING FATS

Eating fats helps provide a slow sustained release of energy, meaning fewer dips and spikes in blood sugar levels. This can make a huge difference when it comes to getting a good night's sleep.

Fatty acids are essential for health and particularly important for growing babies.

Most of the nervous system—the brain, spinal column, and all the nerves that branch out from there, are largely made from fat. Without enough of it, our brains don't develop as well, and this can impact everything from memory and concentration to IQ.

Fatty acids are part of every cell of the body. They help make cell walls flexible and are involved in hormone production, brain development, memory, and concentration. Fatty acids help keep skin smooth, supple, and moisturized. We need them for good vision and to transport essential fat-soluble vitamins to our cells. Certain fatty acids (such as those in flaxseed oil) help to increase cellular metabolism, aiding in

weight loss, while others are involved in building a healthy immune system.

Some (including coconut oil) even have antiviral and antibacterial properties. Fats also slow down the rate at which food leaves the stomach and results in a more sustained release of energy and fewer dips and spikes in blood sugar levels. This can make a huge difference when it comes to getting a good night's sleep. If your child has a nourishing diet with adequate fats, proteins, and micronutrients, he or she is more likely to sleep for longer blocks of time.

There are many types of fats (many more than are listed here), each with different functions.

Unadulterated, natural saturated fats are equally important to have in the diet, so don't shy away from them.

Here's the lowdown

- All oils must be extra-virgin and cold-pressed (no heat-treated extraction processes).
- All liquid oils need to be kept in airtight (preferably glass) containers, jars, or bottles to prevent them from oxidizing or going rancid.
- Some oils *must* be refrigerated in airtight bottles. These include flax, walnut, pumpkin, and hemp seed oil. These oils are polyunsaturated, so they are very unstable and become

rancid with exposure to heat and light. This means that while they have great health benefits when they are fresh, they will cause a lot of free radical damage if they are not stored correctly.

- Cook only with saturated fats, as they are stable at high temperatures.

Good cold-pressed oils to use raw

(For dressings, smoothies, etc.—make sure they are extra-virgin and cold-pressed)

- Flaxseed (store in fridge)
- Hemp seed (store in fridge)
- Olive
- Pumpkin (store in fridge)
- Walnut (store in fridge)

Good fats to use for cooking

- Animal fats: drippings from roasts, lard, tallow, etc. (only from organically and/or pasture-raised animals)
- Coconut oil
- Sesame oil mixed with coconut oil

What to avoid

- All vegetable oil spreads, such as those made with olive oil or canola oil. They may have some fancy names but these oils have been partially hydrogenated—a process that creates both oxidized and trans fats. Trans fats are quickly assimilated into cell membranes, but the cell is unable to use the altered form of the fat and so dysfunction ensues. Cancer and cardiovascular disease are just two diseases that can be linked to trans fats. When margarines and vegetable oil spreads hit the market, the rates of these diseases skyrocketed.

- Anything that is simply labeled "vegetable oil" or "cooking oil."
- Foods fried in unsaturated oils.
- Margarine. If you look into how margarine is made, it will be enough to put you off for life. It's certainly not food.
- Processed foods containing hydrogenated or partially hydrogenated oils.
- Soybean oil, corn oil, canola oil, safflower oil, sunflower oil, and rice bran oil as they are all unstable oils and likely to be heat treated and partially hydrogenated. Soybeans, corn, and canola are also likely to be genetically modified.
- Any foods containing the above oils.

So go to your pantry and fridge and throw out any margarine and any processed (heated) vegetable oils. If you don't like throwing out food, just remember that it's not really "food"—just edible food-like products that are damaging your health and that of your baby!

Fats and the cholesterol myth

Fats and cholesterol are both lipids but have very different functions. Fats provide energy, while cholesterol is a component of every cell in our bodies.

Cholesterol is a greatly misunderstood compound. We're taught we have "good cholesterol" and "bad cholesterol," but in reality there is only one type—the variation lies in the kind of transport molecules that move cholesterol around the body. LDL (low-density lipoproteins) and HDL (high-density lipoproteins) are the molecules that transport cholesterol to and from the liver. LDLs transport cholesterol from the liver and circulate through the bloodstream to deliver it to different cells in the body. HDLs transport cholesterol back to the liver to be either recycled or used to make bile. If LDL cannot bind to LDL receptors (due to low thyroid hormone), then bundles of LDL and cholesterol can build up in the lining of blood vessels. Then, just as oil goes rancid if you leave it exposed to air, these "bundles" become oxidized, causing inflammation and damage to the cells in the vessel wall.

KEY NUTRIENTS FOR BABIES

The first twelve months of life involve astonishingly rapid growth and development. From the onset of labor, a newborn enters into a variable and foreign environment. They move from having every aspect of life heavily regulated in the uterus, to being in a world with changes in temperature and light, where they feel both hunger and satiety. In this period, all of your baby's organs and systems must adapt to an ever-changing environment. Try to imagine this process, in which incredible stress is brought upon us so suddenly! This stress provides a very important opportunity to adapt. As humans, throughout life we are exposed to stressors (without them we'd be dead!), and we must either remove ourselves from the stress or adapt to cope, and even thrive, in its presence.

Most of our cholesterol is manufactured endogenously (in the body). Most cells in the body produce the cholesterol they require. Cholesterol is also derived from animal fats in the diet. No vegetarian fats contain any cholesterol. An increase in dietary intake does not reduce endogenous production to the same degree of intake.

Methods of improving serum cholesterol quality (and improving the ratio of HDL to LDL) include:

- Increasing antioxidant intake, particularly of coenzyme Q10 (heart is the best source)
- Increasing vitamin E intake

- Reducing polyunsaturated fatty acid intake, which easily oxidizes
- Increasing LDL receptor function (by optimizing thyroid function), supporting liver and gall bladder function (to produce more bile)
- Increasing intake of nicotinic acid (vitamin B3)
- Reducing your intake of sugars and starches

Optimum nutrition is crucial not only for your baby's immediate health, but also for his or her health in adulthood, so we must strive to provide foods for babies that will positively affect their metabolic programming well into their adult lives. What a gift to be able to give! Think back to your own life, diet, and relationship with food. So many people have unhealthy relationships with food, developing eating disorders and associated physical illnesses. What if you could help your own child to avoid such struggles by nourishing them with the most nutrient-dense foods right from the beginning? That's not to say they'll never have any health issues, but it would certainly minimize the chances. For example, we know that babies fed on predominantly high-carbohydrate foods, particularly those with a high glycemic index, have a higher incidence of increased insulin production, which predisposes them to weight gain, insulin resistance, and diabetes in adulthood. Animal studies show that this also impacts subsequent generations, so gifting your new baby with nutrient-dense foods means laying a metabolic foundation for your grandchildren as well. Let's get back to thriving as a species!

Fats

Fat intake for babies and toddlers is estimated to be around 50 percent of energy intake.

A high intake of fatty acids—in particular arachidonic acid (AA) and docosahexaenoic acid (DHA)—helps babies to develop a healthy nervous system, cognition, vision, and immune function, protecting them from developing asthma, upper respiratory tract infections, and allergic rhinitis (hay fever). The intake of fatty acids eicosatetraenoic acid (EPA) and DHA is also associated with childhood mental health.

As we saw earlier, cholesterol is crucial for brain development and hormone production. Along with DHA, cholesterol is essential for building myelin, which is like insulation for nerves. Myelin allows information to travel quickly along the nerves from one part of the brain or body to another. It's no coincidence that eggs are high in cholesterol—nature knows that the potential life that comes from an egg is going to need a lot of cholesterol to develop into a healthy chicken.

Fats also provide fat-soluble vitamins A, D, E, and K (all essential for development), and improve the absorption of minerals. Calories from fat are protein sparing, allowing babies to use protein for growth, rather than for energy production.

Choline

Choline often misses out on getting a mention when it comes to discussing pregnancy, breastfeeding, and infancy, yet it is vital for both neurological development and the metabolic processes that ensure healthy cell growth and replication (it directly affects our DNA and RNA production).

Choline also protects a developing child's brain against toxin exposure. The best sources of choline are breast milk, egg yolks, and liver. Nuts, fish, and sunflower lecithin are also useful sources.

A mother's choline levels tend to become depleted during pregnancy and breastfeeding, so it's super important for moms to have regular choline intake in their diet.

Protein

Protein is a crucial nutrient, especially during times of growth and repair. Considering the vast amount of growth that is occurring at this age, good-quality protein will help develop a happy, healthy, and strong child.

Protein is also a vehicle for uptake of zinc, which is a hugely important mineral essential for development of the nervous system, the gut, the immune system, and the endocrine (hormone) system, to name a few. Zinc is eliminated via the bowels, so if your baby has chronic diarrhea, chances are that zinc levels will be easily depleted. One of the most common causes of diarrhea in babies is dairy. If you simply remove dairy from your baby's diet, you may find your baby experiences their first well-formed poop!

Iron

Iron is incredibly important for neurological development. Inadequate iron intake can result in lower IQ and reduced social development in babies and young children. The effects of iron deficiency in infancy can be irreversible, so it's really important to ensure iron-rich foods are part of your diet, and your baby's once he or she starts on solids.

Too much iron is not a good thing either, so please see a health-care provider for blood tests and advice on supplementation.

Because iron is so crucial, Mother Nature has carefully planned for a newborn to have enough iron stores to fulfill their developmental needs until four to six months of age. That is why it is important to start solids around this time. Once solids are introduced, animal sources provide the best-absorbed form of iron, with liver being the greatest source. You actually absorb iron from animal sources two or three times more readily than iron from plants.

Vitamin C increases the absorption of iron, too, so ensure that vitamin C–rich foods (such as sauerkraut juice and eventually fermented veggies) are included in menu planning. Fortunately liver also provides an excellent source of vitamin C, covering both bases! Even the very conservative CDC (Centers for Disease Control) states that babies given milk before the age of twelve months, or who have a diet high in dairy, are at risk of iron deficiency, among other health risks.

Iodine

Iodine is crucial for your baby's development, too. Iodine deficiency is actually the leading cause of preventable intellectual deficiency. The best sources of iodine come from the sea, particularly from kelp, seafood, and good-quality sea salt (usually grayish in color and damp in appearance). Egg yolks are also a good source of this mineral.

Fiber

Fiber is a very important dietary inclusion. It's not only a bit of a broom for the intestines, helping keep our insides clean, it's also an important food source for the microbes that inhabit the gut. When bacteria in our gut have a fiber feast, they end up producing hugely valuable short-chain fatty acids as a result.

These fatty acids are then used to feed the cells that line the bowel wall, keeping them (and therefore your immune system) healthy and happy. Excellent sources of fiber include yams, sweet potatoes, green leafy veggies, carrots and other root vegetables (cooked, raw, and fermented), fruits with an edible peel (where most of the fiber is), and berries, nuts, and seeds.

Calcium

The first source of calcium is breast milk. Once on solids, there are plenty of sources of calcium that can be included in the diet. Bone broths made from bones simmered for twenty-four hours in water with a little vinegar (sounds weird, tastes delicious) is one valuable source. Others include seaweed, figs, sardines, turnip greens, broccoli, kale, blackstrap molasses, artichoke, okra, collard greens, kale, bok choy, and sesame seeds.

Most importantly, calcium must be consumed along with magnesium, vitamin D, and saturated fats to be well absorbed and metabolized.

Without these other nutrients, you will absorb very little calcium. Plant chemicals called phytates in legumes and grains block the absorption of calcium. Any seeds or nuts should also be soaked (activated) prior to eating to deactivate the phytates in these foods.

ABOUT BUGS

When speaking about any aspect of health, it is impossible (or at least incomplete) to do so without talking about bugs—and good bacteria is especially important at this age of development. When talking bugs, think bacteria, yeast, viruses, and parasites.

Here's the fascinating part—we are outnumbered 10:1 by microbes. For every human cell in our bodies, there are ten times as many microbial cells, the vast majority of them in our gut. There's also one hundred times more of their genetic material in us and on us than there are human cells. Yet, without this huge number of microbes we wouldn't be able to live. That's because we live in symbiosis (a mutually rewarding relationship), and when we provide good real estate for them, they carry out hundreds, if not thousands, of functions for us.

The healthy bug population of the human gut acts as a physical barrier between us and the external environment. The digestive tract is actually classified as being outside of the body. Think of a donut—the hole in the donut is still the outside of the donut, and the tube that runs through us is also on the outside.

As a result, most of our immune system is in the gut as well, working hard to protect us from invaders and substances that may jump the fence and get inside.

Our bugs provide a first line of defense against pathogenic organisms in the digestive tract.

Gut bugs also produce enzymes, vitamins—especially B vitamins and biotin—minerals, and polyunsaturated fatty acids. They aid in the predigestion of foods, regulate cholesterol metabolism, and perform major hormone, nervous system, and immune functions.

In utero, a baby's digestive tract is 100 percent sterile. Inoculation of the gut begins at birth, so the type of birth heavily affects what kind of bugs are going to be the first settlers. These first settlers can end up providing a bit of a microbial blueprint for the rest of our lives. During vaginal delivery, the baby's intestinal microflora is predominantly derived from the mother's vaginal, intestinal, and perianal microflora. Children born by cesarean section have significantly different counts of fecal bacterial species, most notably an absence of Bifidobacterium and a delay in their colonization. This is likely a result of bypassing exposure to the mother's microflora through the vagina as well as the use of prophylactic antibiotics. Babies born by C-section receive their gastrointestinal microflora from the delivery room environment.

Breastfeeding also affects the diversity of microbial species in a baby's gut flora. Around 60 to 90 percent of the bugs in a breastfed baby's poop are Bifidobacteria—the predominant bacteria in a healthy infant's gut. This is largely a result of the presence of the types of sugars in breast milk (oligosaccharides)—a favored food source of Bifidobacteria—as well as from skin-to-skin contact with the mother. The microbial balance of formula-fed infants is largely dependent on the type of formula being used. Intestinal microbiota becomes more complex with the introduction of solids, but it has been shown that the quality of the initial inoculation at birth is a pre-determining factor for future microbial colonization in the gut.

The upshot is that babies who are delivered by C-section have higher incidences of immune problems such as asthma and eczema, and this is due to the differences in gut flora. Digestive problems such as colic, reflux, diarrhea, and constipation are also signs that gut bugs need a push in the right direction.

WHY BREAST MILK IS SO SPECIAL

For the first six months of a child's life there's no argument that breast is best, so if it works for you, make the most of it. Not only is breast milk the most nutritious, immune-boosting, brain-developing food you can possibly feed your baby, it also requires no sterilization of bottles or pre-planning for trips away from the house— it's the ultimate food on the go!

Of course, breastfeeding is not always possible, even with the very best intentions.

Why do boobs have it all?

All mammals make milk for their babies. Each species makes a unique formula of milk that is specific to the developmental needs of their young. This is known as the biological specificity of milk.

Human breast milk is primarily composed of fats, cholesterol, and milk sugars, which are crucial for neural and visual development (our greatest priority). It has a relatively small amount of protein compared to the milk of other mammals such as cows, whose priority is growth. The higher protein levels in cow's milk is one reason why human babies have so much trouble digesting it.

Breast milk also contains a host of immune factors including colostrum, lactoferrin, and immunoglobulins. These all help develop your baby's immune system, reducing the frequency and severity of infections and the incidence of allergic and inflammatory conditions later down the track, such as asthma, hay fever, and eczema.

Since babies' intestines are immature and essentially "leaky" in nature, it's important that they get nutrition from easily digestible sources. Breast milk not only contains the right nutrients but also the enzymes required to digest it. For example, due to its high fat content, breast milk comes with a good dose of lipase—an enzyme that breaks down fat, making it super easy for babies to digest and get all the goodness out of it. While the fore milk (the first milk that a baby gets at each feed) is reasonably low in fat, the hind milk provides a nice rich fatty dessert. Repeat feeds in short succession will provide more fat. With space between feeds, the fat content of a feed can drop again. Breast milk also comes equipped with a range of hormones and proteins which actually help to close up the leaky gut of a newborn, making it more impermeable to pathogens and other potentially harmful agents.

BREASTFEEDING ISN'T JUST FOR BABIES

According to the American Dietetic Association, breastfeeding is associated with improved maternal outcomes, including a reduced risk of breast and ovarian cancer, type 2 diabetes, and postpartum depression.

It is recommended that breastfeeding be the exclusive source of nutrition for the infant up to six months of age, and then continued as part of a diet including solid foods up to at least twelve months of age. When you wean is a matter of choice and health. Some mothers practice baby-led weaning, only weaning at a point when the baby is clearly ready emotionally and physically, whereas others may need to wean earlier for any number of reasons.

One point I think is very important to make: while we highly encourage breastfeeding for at least twelve to eighteen months, we also acknowledge that there are times when this is possible but not advantageous.

If you are breastfeeding but exceptionally run down and/or are experiencing health issues, you may need to look at weaning sooner than you'd like.

When breastfeeding, you need enough nutritional intake to support both you and your baby, but nature dictates that baby will get the first serving. So if you are not getting enough nutrition for either dietary or health reasons, you will become depleted, which in the end will also affect the quality of your breast milk. So, absolutely, breastfeeding is best, and you should do it for as long as you can, but only when it's beneficial to both you and your baby.

For additional support or help with breastfeeding, contact your local breastfeeding association.

FORMULA

Commercial formula is the only food approved for children under six months of age who cannot be breastfed. For those over six months of age it is a good idea to supplement formula feeds with other nutrient-dense foods suitable for the age-group. Firstly, despite mountains of evidence that the DHA and amino acids present in breast milk are essential to growth and development, these nutrients are still not mandatory ingredients in infant formula. Food sources of amino acids include fish, eggs, dairy, liver, and brain. For infants who are solely formula-fed, cooked organic liver is the most suitable source.

Cholesterol is another component of breast milk necessary for growth and development, yet it is missing from commercial formulas. Cholesterol makes up 10 percent of the weight of total brain fats. It is essential for nerve transmission and as a component of every cell it helps to maintain cell wall fluidity.

Cholesterol is also essential for the production of reproductive hormones, adrenal steroids, vitamin D, and bile salts.

Pasteurization of milk is performed to kill off potential pathogens in the milk. Pasteurization of dairy products also kills the multiple enzymes, such as lactase, needed to digest the components of the milk. This is a primary reason why dairy allergy and intolerance is so common. Pasteurization also denatures the proteins and hardens the calcium, making it more difficult to absorb. We do not recommend using unpasteurized milk as a substitute; rather, we recommend including safe nonallergenic nutrient foods in the diet to provide nutrients like cholesterol and calcium.

Soy-based formulas are best avoided for many reasons. Firstly, soy contains phytoestrogens, which can cause hormone imbalances. Furthermore, a study of fourteen thousand children revealed an association between the development of peanut allergy and the use of soy-based formula. Infants fed soy formula have more reproductive problems and more asthma as adults. Unfermented soy is high in phytates, which block the absorption of essential minerals such as calcium, iodine, and iron (among others). Iodine deficiency leads to hypothyroid function, resulting in goiters.

Even research back in 1990 found a link between infant soy formula consumption and autoimmune thyroiditis in adulthood (present in epidemic rates these days).

INTRODUCING SOLIDS

Chances are prior to six months of age, your baby's digestive system is not yet primed for taking in solid foods. Under rare circumstances, if your baby is not thriving on breast milk, it's best to seek the advice of an integrative medical practitioner. Most of the research indicates that waiting until six months of age to introduce solids is the best insurance against the development of food allergies.

When introducing food to your babies, just remember that they will thrive on much the same foods that grown-ups do! There is no need for special baby cereals and the like. It's really just about preparing real food that is age-appropriate, and in a form that a little person with no teeth and a partially developed digestive system can successfully eat.

Look for signs that your baby is ready to move to solids.

If they are showing interest and watching what you eat, can sit independently, and move their mouth at the sight of food, it's a sign they are ready.

Introduce small amounts of new foods one at a time, ideally a few days apart, so you can see how your baby responds to different foods. That will make it easier to determine whether there are any foods that they react to at all.

It's a good idea to introduce the first foods after a shortened breast or bottle feed, so that your baby is not ravenously hungry when they try their first food.

It's also a good idea to thin down their first foods by mixing in some breast milk, formula, or baby-building broth, so that it's a consistency that is easy for them to digest.

Let your baby guide you on how much. Once they lose interest or refuse the food, that meal is finished. A teaspoon or two may be enough at first. Ensure your infant or toddler is always supervised while eating.

While solids are generally introduced around the six-month mark, it's advisable to continue breastfeeding to at least one year, or longer if possible.

6+ months

- Egg yolk—if tolerated, preferably from organic pastured chickens, boiled until egg whites are cooked through (whites are not to be consumed until 1 year) and yolk begins to thicken.

- A teaspoon of thickened egg yolk to start.
- Cod liver oil—¼ teaspoon of high-vitamin, or ½ teaspoon regular, given with an eyedropper. Must be guided by integrative medical practitioner.
- Juice from fermented vegetables—¼ teaspoon to start per day. Start out very slowly.
- Bone broth—to cook baby's veggies and meats in. The broth supplies added nutrients and improved digestibility. Start with a small amount, like 30–50 milliliters (or when your baby says enough!). You can even mix in with some expressed breast milk.
- Pureed slow-cooked meats—lamb, turkey, beef, chicken, liver
- Soup broth—chicken, beef, lamb, fish, added to pureed meats and vegetables, or offered as a drink
- Fermented foods—small amounts (¼ teaspoon) of fermented veggie juice, fermented sweet potato, or taro

- Raw mashed fruits—banana, avocado, and tropical fruits
- Cooked, pureed fruits—small amounts of organic apricots, peaches, pears, apples, cherries, berries
- Cooked pureed vegetables—zucchini, squash, sweet potato, carrots and beets, cooked with bone broth and coconut oil

Starting solids is fun and can be messy. Remember a baby's tummy is tiny, so start with only a few mouthfuls then gradually add more solids as required.

8–12 months

- Pureed vegetable soups—made with a bone broth base; add organic lard or tallow for extra fats
- Homemade stews with bone broth base—all ingredients cut small or mashed
- Finger foods—when baby can grab and adequately chew, such as lightly steamed veggie sticks, avocado chunks, pieces of banana

---

1 Sprouted nuts and seeds, also known as "activated," simply means the nuts and or seeds are soaked in highly salted filtered water for a desired amount of time (each nut and seed requires different soaking times, see p. 246), and this soaking process helps to remove much of the irritants that are contained in nuts and seeds so they are less problematic on the digestive system. Once they are soaked for the desired amount of time, they are simply rinsed thoroughly and drained and are ready to be eaten or used in the recipes.

- Cod liver oil—increase to ½ teaspoon high-vitamin or 1 teaspoon regular. (Must be supported by integrative medical practitioner.)

8–12 months
- Continue to add variety and increase the thickness and lumpiness of the foods already given.

12 + months
- Activated nut and seed butters— if tolerated, including chia (we recommend no whole nuts until three years of age to prevent choking hazard). Leafy green vegetables— cooked
- Raw salad vegetables and fruits— cucumbers, tomatoes, etc.
- Citrus fruits—fresh, organic
- Whole egg—cooked
- Fresh or frozen organic berries

WALKING THE WALK

It is important to remember that kids learn from repetition and observation. They will learn more by watching what you do and how you react to foods than they will from what you say. If your child is your motivation for changing the way you eat and how you feed your family, be conscious of approaching new foods with a fun and positive attitude.

Make the preparation and eating of food a nourishing and joyful adventure. Approach it with an open and curious mind, and you will be encouraging your baby (and older kids) to do the same. Make sure both parents are on board with this, as it doesn't work if one of you screws up your face and says "Ugh! I am *not* eating that!" The child will learn that behavior, based on these reactions, and often reject foods that they would otherwise enjoy and be happy to eat!

Kids learn to be open to new flavors by repeated exposure. Remember that every taste and texture to them is an utterly new sensation, so keep offering foods, and be supportive and encouraging.

Also, your baby up to this point has only ever sucked as a way of taking in food. Her reflex is to push her tongue out, so even though it appears that she is pushing food out (and you may assume she doesn't like the taste), it is in fact a very new skill to learn, which can sometimes take time.

FUSSY EATING

Fussy eating is often a sign of an upset in the natural balance of microorganisms in the gut (gut dysbiosis), or a sign that your baby requires more of specific nutrients. Even though it may seem impossible to get fussy eaters to eat fermented veggies, I find this to be one of the best ways to open up their palates to new foods. Give it a go, and remember, being creatures of repetition, the rule of ten applies. Studies show that parents often give up at around five attempts (understandably so), whereas ten seems to be the magic number. Persistence pays off; just be sure to persist in a positive, calm manner to avoid building resistance against new foods.

PREPARATION IS KEY

Having a well-prepped kitchen and well-stocked pantry is essential for providing yourself and your baby with nourishing food. It's when you don't have any pre-prepped meals or versatile, nutrient-dense ingredients ready that things tend to fall off the wagon. Refer to our useful guides at the back of this book for what to keep on hand in your pantry, fridge, and freezer.

PART 1

BABY FOOD

There really is no greater gift to give your children than love, nourishment, encouragement, and connection. This of course can take many forms, and I view food as one of these that cannot be overlooked or understated. By nourishing your little ones with nutrient-dense food that tastes delicious and expands their palate to be adventurous, we are setting our next generation with a solid foundation on which they can build on through their unique and wondrous lives.

BABY BUILDING BROTH

This is one of the most important recipes you can learn to make for your baby and is the hero of this recipe book. It can be added to almost anything you are cooking.

Making broth has been a regular practice in many peoples' cultures for millennia. It's a wonderfully simple way to sneak nutrition into kids' everyday meals. As a cook you feel like you are nourishing them with every mouthful. Is there any better feeling?

Broths are incredibly healing and supportive to the intestinal tract. They aid digestion and are high in magnesium, silicon, calcium, and glucosamine. Broths also make everything taste delicious and at the end of the day can really turn your day around.

It's important for *you* to stay well-nourished and rested too—so please make sure you enjoy a cup of broth as well!

Broth is really useful for fussy little eaters as you can pop it into their food without them knowing it. Let's just keep it our little secret—they can thank us later when they're all big and strong. Use a little to fry up sausages and meats, add a splash to scrambled eggs, Bolognese, and curries. The list is endless.

Making broth is an absolute must-do each week. It's the base for your "hour of power" in the kitchen and is easy-peasy. So, let's get brothing.

MAKES 1 GALLON (4 L)

Prep time: 10 minutes   **Cook time:** 6–12 hours   **Allergens:** none

3 pounds, 5 ounces (1.7 kg) bony
  chicken parts (necks, backs,
  breastbones, and wings)
2–4 chicken feet, *optional*
5¼ quarts (5 l) filtered water
2 tablespoons apple cider vinegar
Veggies such as celery, garlic, leek,
  carrots, pumpkin, sweet potato, or
  taro (for babies 6 months and older)

1. Place the chicken pieces in a stockpot or large saucepan. Add the filtered water and the vinegar (to help draw out the minerals). Bring to a boil, continuously skimming off the skin and foam that forms on the surface of the liquid.

2. Reduce the heat to low and simmer for 6 to 12 hours. The longer you cook the broth, the more the flavors will develop. If you are after a super-flavorsome broth, first brown the bones in a pan with a little coconut oil before adding them to the water.

3. If you are making a broth with veggies, add them in at the last hour of cooking time.

4. Allow the broth to cool slightly before straining it through a fine sieve. Set aside the vegetables and use them for a "super mash."

5. Pour the broth into glass jars, mason jars, or mini silicone molds (use medical-grade silicone). Be sure to leave an inch or so at the top of the glass jars to allow for settling and for fats to solidify.

6. Cover and place the broth in your refrigerator.

7. A fat layer will form at the top when it is cooled—this is great for cooking your meats and veggies in, so skim it off and keep it—don't throw it out!

8. The broth can be stored in the fridge for up to 4 days or frozen for up to 3 months.

9. Date the broth going into the fridge. If kept refrigerated for longer than 4 days, bring it back to a boil before using. Don't use the broth past 5 days.

(6 TO 12 MONTHS)

Notes:

- You will need a large pot/slow cooker/saucepan—ideally without Teflon, as we don't want any potential toxins involved. Cast iron or steel is perfect.

- It's important to not use tap water (unless you have a well), as it's filled with metals that can accumulate when heated. You don't want the heavy metals and fluoride. Remember, it's our job to protect our little ones from toxins.

- It's easy to substitute lamb or beef for the chicken bones: simply use 1 pound (500 g) of lamb or beef soup bones instead of chicken bones. It's okay if your butcher leaves a little meat on the bones, as this is perfect for using in the meat puree. You can even make a broth from cooked carcasses over a few weeks. After roasting a chicken, pop the cooked carcass of the bird in the freezer, and when you have several in there, you are ready to broth.

- In your large pot or slow cooker, use whatever bones you have on hand. Just to be clear—there are no rules, so experiment to your heart's content! Using the feet and necks produces the most wobbly broth, a sure sign it is loaded with gelatin. Let's face it, if you've got a leftover carcass after a roast and you don't want to waste it, you just go for it. Better to broth than not. Experiment with the amount of bones. The more bones the wobblier the broth.

- Always keep some frozen broth in the freezer in little pods (from the silicone molds). It's great to take when traveling as the perfect quick-nourishing meal, or for daycare bags. Just be sure to insist the broth is not heated in the microwave as a rule. Microwaves, although considered convenient, deplete the food of minerals and enzymes—and we want all those goodies in your little ones' bellies.

- Did you know broth is a wonderful way to improve overall family health, heal gut sensitivities, and help digestion issues? It's a fabulous anti-inflammatory, and nature's penicillin. Remember how Grandma's soup always made you feel better? She was on to something good, that's for sure!

HAPPY TUMMY BROTH

This tummy brew can provide a real option for getting a nutrient-dense drink into your baby.

As the Australian National Health and Medical Research Council advises, liver is a great first food for infants from around six months of age. A true superfood, it is rich in iron, zinc, choline, Vitamin A, and B vitamins. Because liver is so wonderfully nutrient dense, use either this or a pâté (choose one or the other, rather than both in a single day).

This nourishing tummy brew is based on a recipe originally formulated by world-renowned nutritional biochemist Dr. Mary Enig—a recipe that has been shared around the world millions of times over. This recipe has been adjusted significantly, to reduce the liver content and to ensure it is as hypoallergenic as possible.

Due to the high rate of neurological growth in babies, having sufficient and a variety of fats is crucially important, so it's imperative to include the coconut oil. The coconut oil is the only ingredient that provides the medium-chain saturated fats that are also present in mother's milk.

We recommend using this recipe once per day and seeking medical advice to learn more.

MAKES ¾ CUP (1 SERVING)

Prep time: 5 minutes   **Cook time:** 5–7 minutes   **Allergens:** none

¼ oz (6 g) organic free-range chicken or lamb liver
¾ cup (6¼ oz/185 ml) Baby Building Broth (page 2) or Chicken Bone Broth (page 33)
½ serving probiotic (suitable for babies and infants)
1 teaspoon organic virgin coconut oil
¼ teaspoon organic extra-virgin olive oil
¹/₈ teaspoon unflavored high-vitamin fermented cod liver oil (such as Green Pastures or Rosita)
¹/₈ teaspoon (1.5 g) 100% pure calcium citrate powder (e.g., Now Foods) equal to 52.5 milligrams calcium
¹/₁₆ teaspoon (tiny pinch) acerola powder

1. Before preparing the Happy Tummy Broth, ensure you always wash your hands and have effective refrigeration, clean surroundings and cooking utensils, and satisfactory arrangements for sterilizing and storing equipment. Ensure previously used bottles and nipples have been thoroughly cleaned. Utensils and bottles can be sterilized using a steam sterilizer or by boiling them in water for 5 minutes.

2. Simmer the liver gently in broth until cooked through; do not overcook. Place the broth and cooked liver in the blender and liquefy. Be careful to blend it thoroughly until smooth, as you don't want it getting stuck inside the bottle's nipple. When the mixture has cooled slightly, add all the other ingredients and blend thoroughly.

(6 TO 12 MONTHS)

Notes:

- You will need an excellent blender. Vitamix or Thermomix are perfect for this.

- Bioceuticals baby biotic is dairy-free and a good general one for babies, otherwise for specific advice, consult your health-care practitioner/naturopath/nutritionist. Another option is qiara—a probiotic made from human breast milk.

- Once a week or every two weeks you can separate the liver into ¼-ounce (6-g) pieces. You can always ask your butcher to do this if you are buying in bulk. Freeze the separate portions, then each night before going to bed take one ¼-ounce (6-g) portion out of the freezer and place in the fridge to slowly defrost overnight. It's ready to use first thing the next morning. A great tip is to label and date the liver portions that you pop in the freezer and remember to always keep cooked and uncooked food in the freezer separately.

- You can also make up several big batches of the broth. That way you have enough for the week in the freezer, and it's less time-consuming. Initially this may seem daunting, but after a few weeks you will be able to prep the tummy brew in a matter of minutes.

- The best way to store the tummy brew is in a sterilized airtight glass jar, and it must be refrigerated. A blender (that detaches from the base) with an airtight seal works well. Make the tummy brew daily for one day's use only. The brew must be stored at 40°F/5°C or below and used within 24 hours. Before you are ready to make a bottle, you can quickly reblend the tummy brew, then pour into a smaller sterilized glass bottle with nipple and warm gently. Sometimes the coconut oil hardens up when refrigerated so the quick blending is really just troubleshooting any later problems. Never use a microwave to reheat. It's best to warm the bottle gently in hot water or a bottle warmer. Always check the temperature before feeding.

- Always ensure brew is served in sterilized nontoxic bottles. Any brew that has been at room temperature for longer than 1 hour should be discarded.

SIMPLE PÂTÉ

Pâté is a superfood for babies—it's so dense in nutrients and is a wonderful first food. It is safe to include pâté in an infant's diet from six months onward—just ensure the meat is from organic, pasture-raised, hormone- and chemical-free animals. You will get the added benefits of high omega-3s as well.

SERVES 6

Prep time: 5 minutes   **Cook time:** 10 minutes   **Allergens:** none

1 tablespoon cold-pressed, virgin coconut oil

1 pound (450 g) free-range chicken, grass-fed beef, or lamb liver, sinew removed

2 cloves garlic, peeled, *optional*

1½ cups (350 ml) Baby Building Broth (page 2) or Chicken Bone Broth (page 33)

Notes:

* Serving this to your child 1 or 2 times a week is recommended.

* Remember, this food is extremely nutrient dense. A few mouthfuls to start is perfect.

* For an adult version, add more garlic, some mustard seeds, and herbs. Delicious!

1. Heat the coconut oil in a saucepan over medium heat. Add the liver and garlic along with 1 cup (240 ml) of the broth and simmer on stove for 8 minutes. Add more broth if it appears to be getting too dry.

2. Once cooked through, carefully transfer the liver, garlic, and juices to a heat-stable food processor and blend on high to a thick and smooth consistency.

3. Cool completely before serving. The remaining pâté can be stored in the refrigerator for up to 3 days, or divided into serving portions in pods or glass jars. You can freeze this pâté for up to 3 months.

(6 TO 12 MONTHS)

BRAIN FOOD PUREE

Organ meats are pure superfood! Compared to muscle meats, organs are richer in just about every nutrient, including phosphorous, iron, copper, magnesium, iodine, B_1, B_2, B_6, folic acid, and vitamin B_{12}. The trick is finding ways to incorporate them into your baby's diet.

Brains are a delicious and nutritious option to include in the diet. The most common brains available are lamb or sheep brains and are famous in many cultures around the world. You can substitute cow or goat brains if you cannot find lamb brains.

SERVES 3–4

Prep time: 5 minutes   **Cook time:** 10 minutes   **Allergens:** none

4 lamb's brains
1½ cups (350 ml) Baby Building Broth (page 2) or Chicken Bone Broth (page 33)
½ cauliflower head, chopped
Zest of 1 lemon
1 tablespoon cold-pressed, extra-virgin olive oil
Juice of ½ lemon

1. Soak the brains in a bowl of filtered water for a couple of hours, or overnight. Drain and rinse, then gently peel off any skin or membrane.

2. Place the bone broth, brains, and cauliflower in a saucepan over medium-high heat and bring to a boil. Reduce the heat to a simmer, cover with a lid, and cook for 15 minutes until the cauliflower is nice and tender. Drain, reserving the broth.

3. Place the brains and cauliflower in a blender with the lemon zest and puree until smooth. (Add a little of the reserved cooking liquid if needed). Allow to cool. When lukewarm, top with some good quality olive oil and add lemon juice.

4. Store the leftovers in a sealed glass jar in the fridge for up to 3 days or in medical-grade silicone containers in the freezer for 3 months.

(6 TO 12 MONTHS)

SWEET POTATO AND PUMPKIN MASH

Mashed, blended, or "smashed" root vegetables are ideal for when first introducing solids. You can cook the veggies in two ways: either by boiling them in Chicken Bone Broth (page 33), or roasting them in the oven.

SERVES 3–4

Prep time: 5 minutes   **Cook time:** 1 hour   **Allergens:** none

1 (about 1 lb/500 g) sweet potato
¼ organic pie pumpkin
2½ cups (600 ml) Baby Building Broth (page 2) or Chicken Bone Broth (page 33), *optional*
1 teaspoon ground cinnamon, *optional*
1 teaspoon cold-pressed, virgin coconut oil, melted

Notes:

- You can make a double or triple quantity of this recipe to create a delicious soup for the adults from the same batch. Separate some for your baby, then to the rest just add a can of organic coconut cream and some grated turmeric and ginger, and top with cilantro.

- The roasted pumpkin skins make a great snack for mom or dad. Don't discard the pumpkin seeds—roast them too, as they are filled with zinc and make for nutritious nibbles while breastfeeding. For a sweet snack, you can drizzle them with a little maple syrup or raw honey—for adults only.

1. If using the boiling-in-broth method, peel and cut the sweet potato and pumpkin into chunks. Place the veggies and broth in a saucepan over medium heat. Bring to a boil and cook for 20 minutes, or until the vegetables can be pierced with a fork. Drain, reserving the broth. Place the vegetables in the blender and process until smooth. Add cinnamon, if using. Serve with cold-pressed, virgin coconut oil and extra broth if needed.

2. To roast the veggies, preheat the oven to 350°F (180°C).

3. Leave the skin on the sweet potato and pumpkin. Cut the pumpkin into two pieces. Place the veggies in a roasting pan with a dollop of broth and the coconut oil. Toss the vegetables before placing them in the oven. Bake for 1 hour, or until golden or soft enough to be pricked easily with a fork.

4. Allow to cool, then remove the skins and set aside. Place the cooked veggies in the blender with the cinnamon (if using) and process until creamy. Feel free to add a little more coconut oil or broth before serving if you want the consistency to be slightly thinner.

(6 TO 12 MONTHS)

FRUITY POWER COMBOS

While these fruit combos are great fun, it is far more important for little developing bodies to get their nutrition from good fats, liver, broth, marrow, and vegetables. Keep these as treats, rather than meals.

SERVES 3–4

Prep time: 5–10 minutes   **Cook time:** 20 minutes   **Allergens:** none

BLUEBERRY AND APPLE SMASH
²/₃ cup (100 g) blueberries
2 apples (red or green), peeled and
    cored

PEAR, BANANA, AND APPLE SMASH
1 pear, peeled and cored
1 banana
1 apple (green or red), peeled and cored

APPLE AND PEAR MASH
1 apple (green or red), peeled and cored
1 pear, peeled and cored

BANANA MASH
2 bananas

1. Place your chosen fruit (except the banana, which can be kept raw) in a saucepan of filtered water. Bring to a boil over high heat. Reduce heat and cook the fruit for 20 minutes or until soft and tender. Drain, reserving some of the liquid.

2. Use a potato masher to mash the cooked fruit until it reaches the desired consistency. Add a little of the reserved liquid if needed. Allow to cool completely before serving.

3. For the Pear, Banana, Apple Smash, mix in the banana once the mash has cooled.

Notes:

- From 8 to 10 months you can begin adding tropical fruits such as papaya that do not need to be cooked first. Tropical fruits are a great addition as they contain so many digestive enzymes, making them a much easier food for babies to digest.

- After 10 months, most other fruits are fine to add, in minimal amounts.

- For a delicious, creamy custard, simply add ¼ cup coconut cream and 1 teaspoon of grass-fed gelatin powder before blending.

(6 TO 12 MONTHS)

MIRACLE MARROW

Marrow is filled to the brim with nutrient-dense fats and is a perfect first food for your baby. Marrow is broken down by the enzyme lipase, which is the same enzyme used to break down breast milk. It makes sense for this to be one of baby's first foods, as it's an easy and natural progression for your child's digestive system.

SERVES 4–5

Prep time: 1 minute   **Cook time:** 15–20 minutes   **Allergens:** none

1 pound (450 g) grass-fed organic marrow bones, cut into 2-inch (5-cm) pieces (you can get your butcher to do this)

1–2 tablespoons Baby Building Broth (page 2) or Chicken Bone Broth (page 33)

1. Preheat the oven to 425°F (220°C).

2. Place the marrow bones in a roasting pan lined with parchment paper. Sprinkle with a little broth. Roast in the oven for 15 to 20 minutes or until cooked through.

3. Allow the marrow bones to cool, then scrape out the marrow and discard the bones. The marrow should be easy to mash with a fork; if it's still dry, give it a few more minutes in the oven or add more broth.

(6 TO 12 MONTHS)

Notes:

- This makes an excellent and highly nutritious puree that keeps for 2 or 3 days in the fridge in a sealed glass container.

- As your child develops, you can try serving marrow with a beautiful pesto or even chimichurri.

PRO-TEENY PUREE

Meat purees provide simple and nutrient-dense meals for growing babies. As a rule, it is best to cook these meats in their own broth following the recipe for Chicken Bone Broth (page 33). Organic chicken, lamb, and beef are fantastic to start with.

SERVES 4

Prep time: 5 minutes   **Cook time:** 3–4 hours (slow cooked)   **Allergens:** none

2 cups (500 ml) Baby Building Broth (page 2) or Chicken Bone Broth (page 33), plus extra if needed
1 pound (450 g) grass-fed beef, organic lamb, or free-range chicken, cut into chunks

Note:

• This recipe will make enough puree to freeze so you always have a meal ready to go.

1. Place the broth in a saucepan over medium-high heat and bring to a boil.

2. Reduce the heat to a simmer and add the meat to the pan. Simmer gently for 3 or 4 hours until the meat is soft and tender. Add more broth if you find that the liquid is reducing too much. (There should always be enough broth to cover the meat when braising.)

3. Remove the pan from the heat and allow to cool slightly. Drain, reserving the liquid. Transfer the braised meat to the bowl of a food processor. Add half of the reserved liquid and blend until pureed. If the puree seems a bit too dry, slowly add a little more broth and process again until it reaches the desired consistency. Check the temperature before serving to ensure it is not too hot for your baby.

4. Store leftovers in sealed glass jars in the fridge for 2 or 3 days, or in medical-grade silicone containers in the freezer.

(6 TO 12 MONTHS)

VEGGIE PUREE COMBOS

Once you get the hang of making the Chicken Bone Broth (page 33), you can start cooking some yummy vegetables in it, creating nutrient-dense dishes in no time. Note that taro takes a little longer to cook than other veggies.

SERVES 2–4

Prep time: 5 minutes   **Cook time:** 20 minutes   **Allergens:** none

2 cups (480 ml) Baby Building Broth (page 2) or Chicken Bone Broth (page 33)
1 heaping tablespoon cold-pressed, virgin coconut oil

6–10 MONTH VEGGIE COMBO OPTIONS
Pumpkin and sweet potato
Beet and carrot
Sweet potato and taro pumpkin and pear

8–10 MONTH VEGGIE COMBO OPTIONS
Broccoli and cauliflower
Celery and leek
Carrot and parsnip
Zucchini, carrot, and pumpkin

1. Wash your chosen vegetables, peel (if necessary), and cut into small pieces. Place them in a small saucepan with the broth. Bring to a boil over medium heat and cook until soft. Drain, reserving the broth.

2. Place the veggies and a dash of broth in a blender and whizz until it reaches the desired consistency. Add more broth if necessary, and a good dollop of coconut oil.

Notes:

- For extra protein, add a handful of chicken meat from the carcass used to make your Happy Tummy Broth.

- You can drink the leftover broth—it's incredibly nutritious.

- Add a sprinkle of dulse flakes. This beautiful seaweed mix is an incredible way to add in even more nutrients, including vitamins A, B_1, B_2, B_3, B_6, B_{12}, C, and E, and other minerals (calcium, potassium, magnesium, phosphorous, chromium, iodine, and zinc).

- The addition of spices and chia seeds is optional around the 10- to 12-month mark and is a great way to develop a baby's palate. Start with cumin, cardamom, nutmeg, and cinnamon.

(6 TO 12 MONTHS)

MUSHIES, BEEF, AND MARROW

Slow-cooked meats are some of my favorite dishes as they have so much more flavor. They are also good value, as they use the cheaper cuts. By cooking meat slowly, you break down its texture so it just melts in the mouth.

SERVES 4–5

Prep time: 10 minutes   **Cook time:** 1 hour 30 minutes   **Allergens:** none

2 tablespoons cold-pressed, virgin coconut oil
½ pound (250 g) grass-fed boneless beef chuck, cut into ¾-inch (2-cm) cubes
½ pound (250 g) beef marrow bones, cut into 2-inch (5-cm) pieces
1 large portobello mushroom, sliced
Handful green beans
1 large carrot, chopped
1 cup (240 ml) Baby Building Broth (page 2) or Chicken Bone Broth (page 33), or water
Pinch freshly ground black pepper

1. Preheat the oven to 325°F (160°C).

2. Melt the coconut oil in a frying pan over medium heat. Add the beef and cook for 4 minutes or until browned on all sides.

3. Meanwhile, pop the marrow out of the bones and slice it into 2-inch (5 cm)-thick pieces. Add to the beef and fry until lightly brown, 30 seconds each side.

4. Transfer the meat, marrow, and pan juices to a small ovenproof dish. Add the mushroom, beans, and carrot and pour over the beef broth or water, if using. Season with pepper, cover the dish with foil or a lid, and bake in the oven for 1½ hours until the meat is tender. (Check after 1 hour to see if more liquid is needed.)

5. Set aside to cool slightly. Coarsely mash, chop, or pulse the beef and vegetables in a food processor and serve warm.

6. Store leftovers in an airtight container in the fridge for 2 or 3 days.

(6 TO 12 MONTHS)

SUPER GUACAMOLE

There's just so much goodness in this little dip. Garlic has antimicrobial properties, while the turmeric and slippery elm powder are anti-inflammatory. Slippery elm powder is made from the inside bark of the slippery elm tree and has a soothing effect on the gastrointestinal tract. It's good for acid reflux, diarrhea, ulcers, and IBS, and is loaded with magnesium, iron, zinc, and vitamins C and B.

SERVES 1–2

Prep time: 5 minutes   **Cook time:** n/a   **Allergens:** none

1 ripe avocado
½ clove garlic, crushed
1 teaspoon chia seeds
1 teaspoon finely chopped cilantro
   leaves
¼ teaspoon ground turmeric
1 teaspoon coconut oil, melted
½ teaspoon slippery elm powder

1. Remove the seed from the avocado. Scoop out the avocado flesh and place it in a bowl. Add the remaining ingredients and mash with a fork.

2. This is a perfect high-fat snack when served with Rosemary Seed Crackers (page 92).

(12+ MONTHS)

SALMON PÂTÉ

Both fresh and canned salmon have health benefits due to their high concentration of omega-3 fatty acids, but salmon canned with the bones also provides a hefty dose of calcium from the edible bones. This recipe is only suitable after 24 months as it contains raw egg yolk in the aïoli.

SERVES 2–4

Prep time: 10 minutes   **Cook time:** n/a
Allergens: fish (suitable for 12+ months only), egg (in the aïoli, if using)

½ pound (230 g) tinned red salmon in brine or olive oil, drained, skin discarded
1 tablespoon lemon juice
½ teaspoon finely grated lemon zest
2 tablespoons homemade Aïoli (page 239)
⅓ cup (90 g) roasted bone marrow (see Mushies, Beef, and Marrow, page 20)
1 teaspoon freshly chopped dill

1. Place all the ingredients in a food processor and blend until very smooth. Taste some to check there are no lumps or fish bones. Season with a little pepper if desired. Serve with celery sticks or a selection of crunchy raw veggies of your choice.

Notes:

- You can also use tinned trout, mackerel, or tuna instead of the salmon.

- If required, you can add 2 tablespoons of filtered water to thin the pâté.

- You can replace the aïoli with 2 tablespoons marrow if you want to include this at 12 months.

(12+ MONTHS)

SARDINE PÂTÉ

Sardines are an excellent source of omega-3 fatty acids and vitamins D and B$_{12}$. They are also one of the most underrated fish and a very sustainable species. Paired with bone marrow, this is a nutrient-dense spread that toddlers will love as a dip once they're old enough for raw veggies and seed crackers.

SERVES 2–4

Prep time: 10 minutes   **Cook time:** n/a
Allergens: fish (suitable for 12+ months only), egg (in the aïoli, if using)

½ pound (230 g) canned boneless sardines in olive oil or spring water, drained
1 clove garlic, crushed
2 tablespoons roasted bone marrow (see Mushies, Beef, and Marrow, page 20), *optional*
2 tablespoons homemade Aïoli (page 239), *optional*
1 tablespoon chopped parsley
½ teaspoon finely grated lemon rind
Juice of ½ lemon
Freshly ground black pepper

1. Place all the ingredients in a food processor and blend until combined. You can blend the pâté until very smooth if that is the texture you desire. Season with a little pepper and serve with cucumber sticks or any raw veggies of your choice.

Note:

• Aïoli contains raw egg yolk and is not recommended in babies' diet until 24 months. If you want to make this recipe before 24 months, use double the amount of marrow.

(12+ MONTHS)

TURMERIC-SPICED CHICKEN

I love these simple recipes that introduce healing spices into our children's diets. This one couldn't be easier or more delicious, and I'm certain it will become your child's favorite.

SERVES 4

Prep time: 10 minutes   **Cook time:** 35 minutes   **Allergens:** none

1 tablespoon cold-pressed, virgin coconut oil
1 small onion, finely chopped
1 clove garlic, finely chopped
1 tablespoon chopped mint leaves
Pinch ground cumin
½ teaspoon ground turmeric or 1 teaspoon grated fresh turmeric
½ pound (250 g) free-range chicken thighs, diced
1 cup (120 g) cauliflower, chopped
1 tomato, chopped
½ cup (125 ml) Chicken Bone Broth (page 33) or filtered water

1. Melt the coconut oil in a frying pan over low heat. Add the onion, garlic, and mint then sauté, stirring often, until the onion is very soft and caramelized (about 8 minutes).

2. Stir in the cumin, turmeric, chicken, and cauliflower and cook for 3 more minutes. Add the tomato and cook until the tomato breaks down to a pulp (about 8 minutes).

3. Pour in the broth or water and simmer until the chicken is completely cooked (about 10 minutes). Transfer to a food processor and process to the desired consistency.

4. Add more broth if needed. Store in an airtight container in the fridge for 2 or 3 days.

(12+ MONTHS)

PART 2
KIDS' MEALS

I am so thrilled to bring you this collection of recipes to include in your cooking repertoire for you and your family. I like to always invite the cook to play around in the kitchen and simply use all the recipes as guides and then feel free to substitute ingredients that are local and seasonal, or simply the ones that you love to cook with, or you can follow the recipes to the letter if that suits you best. Meals are easy to create when you have a well-stocked pantry, fridge, and freezer, and with quality ingredients on hand, even the simplest meals will turn out delicious. Part of sourcing good-quality ingredients is to look into how they are grown, caught, or raised and where they come from.

A great way to get to know where your produce comes from is to get to your local markets and butchers and start the conversation. Let's get back to how things used to be, when people knew where their produce came from and how it had been treated. Finding a great network too can make life a lot easier. Use your "village" or "tribe" to help you on your adventure. Think about batch cooking (making double or more) and swapping with like-minded parents or friends and family so you have wonderful food choices for the week. If you are new to this way of cooking, you can jump in the deep end and change all at once, or simply incorporate these new recipes to suit your family's lifestyle and budget one at a time and slowly build up a beautiful repertoire of dishes that best suit you.

These recipes are intended to be family favorites and will have particular appeal to parents dealing with allergies, asthma, digestive problems, skin issues, and neurological and behavioral disorders.

CHICKEN BONE BROTH

MAKES 4¼ QUARTS (4 L)

Prep time: 10 minutes (plus 1 hour marinating time)
Cook time: 6–12 hours   **Allergens:** none

3⅓ pounds (1.5 kg) bony chicken parts (necks, backs, breastbones, and wings)

2–4 chicken feet, *optional*

2 tablespoons apple cider vinegar

1 large onion, coarsely chopped

2 carrots, coarsely chopped

3 celery stalks, coarsely chopped

2 leeks (white part only), rinsed and coarsely chopped

1 whole garlic bulb, cut in half

2 large handfuls flat-leaf parsley

1 tablespoon black peppercorns, lightly crushed

1. Place the chicken pieces in a stockpot or large saucepan; add 5¼ quarts (5 l) of cold water, the vinegar, onion, carrot, celery, leek, garlic, parsley, and peppercorns and leave to stand for 30 minutes to 1 hour.

2. Bring to a boil, continuously skimming off the skin and foam that forms on the surface of the liquid. Reduce the heat to low and simmer for 6 to 12 hours. The longer you cook the broth, the more the flavors will develop.

3. Allow to cool slightly before straining the broth through a fine sieve into a large storage container.

4. Cover and place in your refrigerator until the fat rises to the top and congeals. Skim off the layer of fat from the top and reserve the fat and broth in covered containers in your refrigerator or freezer. The reserved fat can be used as cooking oil for meat, poultry, and vegetable dishes.

5. The broth can be stored in the refrigerator for up to 4 days or frozen for up to 3 months.

SOFT-BOILED EGGS WITH EGG BREAD SOLDIERS

My daughters absolutely love boiled eggs. And I cannot think of a better way to start their day than with a protein-and-good-fat-packed parcel of goodness. Chop up some herbs, such as chives, dill, or parsley, and sprinkle them over the runny yolk. This egg bread is a great recipe for those people who would like to try a paleo diet but are worried about how they are going to survive without bread. I fully understand the resistance to giving up our daily bread, and with this recipe—kindly shared by my good friends Marlies and Jai from Paleo Café—you won't feel like you are missing out on anything. Try wrapping some jamón or prosciutto around the toast before dipping into the egg.

SERVES 4

Prep time: 20 minutes   **Cook time:** 25–30 minutes   **Allergens:** egg

4 eggs
Coconut oil or ghee, at room
  temperature, to serve

EGG BREAD (MAKES 1 LOAF)
¾ cup (185 ml) coconut oil or ghee,
  melted
15 eggs
½ cup (55 g) flaxseed meal
½ cup (60 g) coconut flour
¾ teaspoon baking powder
¾ teaspoon garlic powder
¾ teaspoon sea salt flakes
¾ teaspoon cracked black pepper

1. To make the egg bread, preheat the oven to 350°F (180°C). Line a 8 × 4-inch (20 × 10-cm) loaf pan with parchment paper.

2. Place the coconut oil or ghee and 10 of the eggs in a large bowl and beat with an electric mixer on high speed for 2 or 3 minutes, or until slightly aerated. Reduce the speed to low and add the flaxseed meal, coconut flour, baking powder, garlic powder, salt, and pepper. Continue beating for another 2 minutes. The mixture will look a bit curdled at this stage, but that's fine.

3. Return the speed to high and add the remaining five eggs one at a time, beating well after each addition, until the mixture is fluffy.

4. Pour the mixture into the loaf pan and bake for 25 to 30 minutes, or until it is lightly browned, and a skewer inserted into the center of the bread comes out clean. Turn the loaf out onto a wire rack to cool.

5. Place the four eggs in a saucepan of cold water, cover, and bring to a boil over high heat. Reduce the heat and simmer for 4 minutes to get lovely, soft yolks.

6. Transfer the eggs to egg cups. Using a spoon, carefully remove the tops from the eggs.

7. Meanwhile, cut four thick slices of egg bread and toast until golden. Spread the toast with some coconut oil or ghee and cut into finger-size portions. Serve immediately with the eggs. The remaining egg bread will keep in an airtight container in the fridge for up to 1 week or in the freezer for up to 3 months.

BACON AND EGGS WITH SLOW-ROASTED CHERRY TOMATOES AND AVOCADO

SERVES 2

Prep time: 10 minutes   **Cook time:** 40 minutes   **Allergens:** eggs

6 cherry tomatoes, cut into halves

½ teaspoon dried oregano

1 clove garlic, crushed

4 tablespoons coconut oil or other good-quality fat, melted, *divided*

Sea salt and freshly ground black pepper

4 slices free-range bacon

4 free-range eggs

½ ripe avocado, cut into ¾-inch (2 cm) cubes

1 teaspoon lemon juice

1 tablespoon olive oil

Flat-leaf parsley leaves, to serve

2 tablespoons cultured vegetables or krauts of your choice (see Beginners' Kraut on page 218)

1. Preheat the oven to 250°F (120°C).

2. Line a baking sheet with parchment paper and arrange the cherry tomatoes, cut-side up, on the prepared sheet. Sprinkle on the oregano and garlic and drizzle 1 tablespoon of the coconut oil or fat over the top. Season with salt and pepper. Bake in the oven for 30 to 35 minutes, or until the tomatoes have shrunk slightly but still appear juicy.

3. Heat 1 tablespoon of the coconut oil or fat in a nonstick frying pan over medium heat, then add the bacon and cook for 2 or 3 minutes on each side until golden. If you like your bacon very crispy, cook for longer. Remove from the pan and keep warm.

4. Wipe the pan clean and reheat over medium heat with the remaining coconut oil or fat. Crack in the eggs and fry for 2 minutes until the egg white is set, or the eggs are cooked to your liking.

5. Place the avocado in a small bowl and pour in the lemon juice and olive oil. Gently toss and set aside. Arrange the bacon and eggs on serving plates, then top with the avocado and oven-roasted cherry tomatoes, and season with salt and pepper.

6. Garnish with the parsley and serve with a tablespoon of cultured vegetables for each serving.

MUSSEL PÂTÉ

Mussels or tinned salmon on their own may be a bit tricky to feed your kids, but when the mussels or salmon are blended with delicious aïoli and lemon, your kids will keep coming back for more. Wait until your child is twelve months to introduce fish or mollusks. This recipe is only suitable after twenty-four months as it contains raw egg yolk in the aïoli.

SERVES 2–4

Prep time: 10 minutes   **Cook time:** n/a   **Allergens:** shellfish, fish, egg

3 ounces (85 g) canned, smoked mussels in olive oil

8¾ ounces (250 g) canned red salmon in brine or olive oil, drained, skin discarded

1 tablespoon lemon juice

½ teaspoon finely grated lemon zest

1 teaspoon chopped parsley

4 tablespoons homemade Aïoli (page 239)

Freshly ground black pepper

1. Place all the ingredients in a food processor and blend until smooth. Season with a little pepper if desired. Serve with Gluten-free Bread (page 223) or raw vegetables.

CHICKEN NUGGETS

Kids just love these little mouthfuls of juicy goodness. This is yummy finger food at its easiest, and a guaranteed crowd-pleaser at parties, sleepovers, and special occasions. Aïoli can be added to this recipe for children over twenty-four months. The aïoli contains raw egg and shouldn't be included beforehand.

SERVES 4–6

Prep time: 15 minutes (plus 1–8 hours marinating)
Cook time: 10 minutes   **Allergens:** egg

1¾ pounds (800 g) free-range organic chicken thighs
2 cloves garlic
2 segments preserved lemon
⅓ cup (80 ml) filtered water
3 teaspoons paprika, *optional*
½ cup (60 g) tapioca flour
freshly ground black pepper
2 organic, free-range eggs, plus 1 egg white
Cold-pressed, virgin coconut oil or duck fat, for frying
Aïoli (page 239), *optional*, to serve

1. Dice the chicken into bite-size nuggets. Crush the garlic and preserved lemon using a mortar and pestle. Transfer to a bowl along with ⅓ cup (80 ml) of filtered water and mix well. Add the chicken nuggets to the garlic and preserved lemon and mix well. Cover and marinate in refrigerator for at least an hour, preferably overnight.

2. Drain the chicken of any excess marinade. In a bowl, mix the paprika (if using) with the tapioca flour and season with pepper. In another bowl, lightly beat the eggs and egg white. Dust each nugget in the tapioca mix, then dip it into the egg mix. Set the coated nuggets aside.

3. Pour 1 inch (2½ cm) of oil into a deep saucepan and place over medium-high heat. Test the temperature by placing a small piece of chicken into the pan; if the oil begins to sizzle, it has reached the ideal heat for shallow-frying. Cook the chicken nuggets in batches for 3 to 5 minutes on each side or until golden brown and the chicken is cooked through. Remove the nuggets from the pan using metal tongs or a slotted spoon, and transfer to a sheet of paper towel to drain off the excess oil. Allow the chicken nuggets to cool slightly before serving with aïoli on the side.

MIGHTY MEATY MUFFINS

Meat muffins are a great way for kids to get their little hands around tasty portions of protein-rich goodness. These are perfect for lunch boxes or a delicious dinner.

SERVES 6

Prep time: 15 minutes   **Cook time:** 15 minutes   **Allergens:** egg, soy (if using)

1 tablespoon cold-pressed, virgin coconut oil or other good-quality fat

2 cloves garlic, finely chopped

1 onion, finely chopped

1 cup (50 g) kale, finely chopped

3 slices free-range, nitrate-free organic bacon

½ cup (125 g) tomato puree

¼ cup (60 ml) coconut aminos

¼ cup (60 ml) chicken or beef broth (page 33 and page 146)

2 teaspoons coconut barbecue sauce or tamari

½ teaspoon garam masala

1 pound (450 g) ground lamb, pork, or grass-fed beef

½ pound (225 g) ground free-range chicken, lamb, or grass-fed beef liver

1 free-range, organic egg

½ cup (80 g) grated carrot

1 teaspoon finely chopped basil

1 teaspoon chopped thyme leaves

1. Preheat the oven to 350°F (180°C). Lightly grease a 12-cup muffin pan with coconut oil. Heat the oil in a pan. Add the garlic, onion, kale, and bacon and sauté until browned.

2. Remove from the heat and set aside.

3. To make the sauce, combine the tomato puree, coconut aminos, broth, barbecue sauce or tamari and garam masala.

4. In a separate bowl combine the meats, egg, carrot, basil, thyme, and half of the sauce. Add the garlic onion, kale, and bacon mixture. Mix together until well combined.

5. Spoon the mixture evenly into the muffin cups. Place a small dollop of sauce on top of each one.

6. Bake in the oven for 12 minutes. Spoon the remaining sauce evenly over the muffins and bake for another 12 minutes. You will have perfectly juicy meaty little muffins. Serve with some mashed veggies and pour over any extra juice from the muffins

Notes:

- Ask your butcher to grind (mince) the liver or you can process it in your blender.

- Coconut barbecue sauce is made with coconut nectar and is a low-GI alternative to the usual stuff. If you can't find it, tamari is fine to use instead.

CHICKEN SCHNITZEL AND CHIPS

SERVES 2–4

Prep time: 15 minutes   **Cook time:** 6–10 minutes   **Allergens:** nuts, egg, sesame

4 free-range, organic chicken thighs

1 cup (100 g) almond meal

2 tablespoons sesame seeds

Zest of ½ lemon

Juice of 1 lemon

Freshly ground black pepper

2 tablespoons arrowroot or tapioca flour

1 free-range, organic egg

2 tablespoons organic coconut milk or almond milk

Cold-pressed, virgin coconut oil, for shallow frying

1. Place the chicken between two sheets of parchment paper and pound with a meat mallet to ⅓-inch (1-cm) thickness.

2. Combine the almond meal, sesame seeds, lemon zest, and juice in a shallow bowl and mix well. Season with a touch of pepper if desired and set aside.

3. Place the arrowroot or tapioca flour in another shallow bowl.

4. In a third bowl, whisk together the egg and coconut or almond milk and set aside. Sprinkle the pounded chicken with the flour, shaking off any excess.

5. Dip each piece of chicken in the egg mixture, then evenly coat with the almond meal mixture.

6. Pour 1 inch (2½ cm) of coconut oil into a large, deep frying pan. Heat the oil over medium-high heat until it reaches around 325°F (160°C). To test, place a tiny piece of chicken into the oil—if it starts to bubble around the chicken immediately, the oil is ready. Fry the crumbed chicken for 3 to 5 minutes on both sides, or until golden and cooked through. Remove from the pan and place on paper towel to drain excess oil.

7. Season with some extra pepper if desired.

8. Serve the chicken schnitzels with Sweet Potato Crisps (page 166) and some Aïoli (page 239).

SALMON PATTIES
WITH GREEN GODDESS DRESSING

Kids love any food they can pick up and interact with, and these little fish patties are a sure winner. They're also packed with protein and good fish oils and are great for lunch boxes. Remember to always use lunch boxes with an ice pack and store appropriately.

SERVES 6

Prep time: 15 minutes   **Cook time:** 15 minutes
Allergens: fish, nuts, egg (suitable for 12+ months only)

1 tablespoon cold-pressed, virgin coconut oil, plus extra for pan-frying

1 onion, finely diced

3 cloves garlic, minced

2 (6-oz/170-g) cans wild salmon

4 free-range, organic eggs, whisked

1 cup (100 g) almond meal

2 tablespoons chopped parsley

1 teaspoon Dijon mustard

Note:

- This dish makes great leftovers. The patties and dressing will keep well in the fridge for 3 or 4 days.

1. Heat 1 tablespoon of coconut oil in a frying pan over medium heat. Add the onion and sauté until soft and translucent (about 5 minutes). Add the garlic and cook for 1 minute. Remove the pan from the heat and allow to cool.

2. In a bowl, combine the onion mixture with the salmon, eggs, almond meal, parsley, and mustard and mix well. Season with pepper.

3. Roll the mixture into 14 balls, then gently press down to flatten into patties around 2⅓ inch (6 cm) in diameter.

4. Heat enough coconut oil to just cover the base of a large frying pan. Fry the patties in batches over medium heat, for 2 to 4 minutes on each side, until golden and cooked through. Drain on paper towels and season with pepper.

5. Serve the patties with Green Goddess Dressing (page 240).

BACON AND ZUCCHINI FRITTERS

These make excellent finger food and will satisfy the hungriest and fussiest little eaters. We love them as lunch box fillers, and they're the perfect snack on the go.

SERVES 6

Prep time: 20 minutes   **Cook time:** 6 minutes   **Allergens:** nuts, egg

Cold-pressed, virgin coconut oil for pan-frying

4 slices free-range, nitrate-free bacon, cut into small pieces

2 cloves garlic, crushed

3 medium zucchinis (about 1 lb/450 g), grated

1 carrot, grated

3 free-range, organic eggs

4 scallions, finely chopped

½ cup (50 g) almond meal or 2 tablespoons coconut flour

1 teaspoon lemon zest

1 tablespoon chopped parsley leaves

1. Heat a teaspoon of coconut oil in a frying pan over medium-high heat. Add the bacon and fry for 2 or 3 minutes or until golden and slightly crispy. Drain on paper towels.

2. Using the same pan, add the garlic and cook for 30 seconds over medium heat until fragrant and soft. Set aside.

3. Place the grated zucchini in a colander over the sink. This will help "sweat" the zucchini and release the liquid. After 10 minutes or so, squeeze all the moisture out with your hands and allow it to drain off. Pat the zucchini dry with a paper towel and transfer it to a bowl.

4. Add the carrot, eggs, scallions, almond meal, lemon zest, and parsley to the bowl of zucchini as well as the bacon and garlic.

5. At this stage it's good to test and cook just one fritter to make sure the mixture holds together well. Form the mixture into a small patty approximately 2½ inches (6 cm) in diameter.

6. Heat the coconut oil in a frying pan over medium heat. When the coconut oil is hot, add the test fritter and cook until golden, turning once (about 4 minutes). If your test fritter does not hold together well, remove the pan from the heat. Add a little more almond meal or coconut flour to the mixture, then form the rest of the patties. Return the pan to the heat and cook all the fritters. Drain them on paper towel.

7. Serve with some halved cherry tomatoes and a sprinkle of fresh basil leaves.

SPECKLED CHICKEN

This is such a fun, yummy (and messy) dinner! Keep some wipes or a warm bowl of water and paper towel on the table for sticky fingers. For a deeper, richer flavor you can marinate the chicken overnight. If you're time-poor, don't worry, as it will be just fine made up moments before eating too. It makes great finger food for children 1½ years or older.

SERVES 3–4

Prep time: 15 minutes (plus 4–12 hours marinating)   **Cook time:** 30 minutes
Allergens: sesame (suitable for 12+ months only), soy (if using tamari)

1¼ pounds (550 g) free-range chicken wings, tips removed

MARINADE
2 tablespoons coconut aminos
2 tablespoons coconut barbecue sauce or tamari
2 cloves garlic, crushed
½ teaspoon ground ginger
¼ cup (60 ml) Chicken Bone Broth (page 33)
2 tablespoons black sesame seeds
2 tablespoons white sesame seeds
¼ cup raw honey or maple syrup
½ teaspoon apple cider vinegar
1 teaspoon grated turmeric

1. Combine all the marinade ingredients in a bowl. Add the chicken wings and use your fingers to give them a good mix. Cover and leave to marinate in the refrigerator (overnight if possible).

2. Preheat the oven to 400°F (200°C).

3. Place the marinated wings in a single layer on a sheet lined with parchment paper. Bake for 30 minutes, turning them after 15 minutes, or until the chicken wings are cooked through and appear golden and sticky.

Notes:

- As this recipe contains honey, we recommend waiting until your child is 12 months to try it.

- Coconut barbecue sauce is made with coconut nectar and is a natural, low-GI alternative to the regular stuff. You can purchase it from a health shop or online, but if you can't find it, just use tamari.

- You can ask your butcher to remove the tips of the wings (keep them for broth making). This makes the wings into little drumettes—lovely and fleshy, and easily handled by little fingers.

CHICKEN AND VEGGIE MUFFINS

The aroma of these tasty morsels baking in the oven will be enough to get your little one's taste buds dancing. They're an ideal snack, breakfast, lunch, or dinner, and you can vary the ingredients to suit your child's preferences. They're also perfect for picnics or school lunch boxes.

SERVES 6–12

Prep time: 15 minutes   **Cook time:** 40 minutes   **Allergens:** egg

1½ tablespoons cold-pressed, virgin coconut oil, melted, *divided*, plus extra for greasing

1⅓ cups (200 g) pumpkin, cut into ⅓-inch (1-cm) cubes

½ teaspoon freshly ground black pepper, *divided*

2 slices (5½ ounces) free-range, nitrate free, rindless bacon or ham, diced

2 cloves garlic, minced

2 scallions, finely chopped

2 cups (70 g) Swiss chard or spinach, chopped

5 free-range, organic eggs

½ teaspoon gluten-free baking soda

1⅓ pounds (600 g) free-range organic ground chicken thigh

1. Preheat the oven to 350°F (180°C). Grease a 12-cup muffin pan with coconut oil.

2. Place the pumpkin cubes on a greased baking sheet. Sprinkle with ¼ teaspoon of the freshly ground black pepper. Drizzle with 1 teaspoon of coconut oil. Roast in the oven for about 12 minutes or until tender.

3. Set aside and allow to cool.

4. Heat the remaining coconut oil in a frying pan over medium heat. Add the bacon and fry for 2 or 3 minutes or until slightly golden. Add the garlic and scallions and cook for a further minute. Add the Swiss chard or spinach and cook until just wilted. Transfer the bacon mixture to a bowl and allow to cool completely.

5. In another bowl, whisk together the eggs, baking soda, and pepper. Add the cooled bacon mixture and ground chicken and mix well with your hands or a wooden spoon.

6. Gently stir in the cooked pumpkin.

7. Spoon the mixture evenly into the muffin tin. Bake for 25 minutes or until the muffins are firm to the touch and cooked through.

8. Remove the muffins from the pan and serve with some raw or cooked veggies of your choice.

BAKED HAM AND EGG CUPS

These are terrific for the whole family and wonderful served with some crispy bacon, avocado, and a side of fermented veggies. Easy and delicious!

SERVES 6

Prep time: 15 minutes   **Cook time:** 20–25 minutes   **Allergens:** egg

1 tablespoon cold-pressed, virgin coconut oil, plus extra for greasing
1 onion, finely chopped
2 cloves garlic, finely minced
6 free-range, organic eggs
½ cup (80 g) chopped red bell pepper
1 zucchini, grated
Freshly ground black pepper
6 slices free-range, organic ham, cut in half
Pinch dulse flakes, *optional*

1. Preheat the oven to 350°F (180°C).

2. Grease a 12-cup muffin pan with a little coconut oil.

3. Heat the coconut oil in a frying pan over medium heat. Add the onion and cook for 2 or 3 minutes until translucent. Add the garlic and cook for a further 40 seconds until fragrant and starting to brown.

4. Whisk together the eggs, peppers, and zucchini and add the cooked onion and garlic. Season with a little cracked pepper.

5. Line each muffin cup with half a ham slice so it almost resembles a cupcake liner. Pour the egg mixture into the ham-lined muffin molds to just below the rim. Sprinkle the tops with dulse flakes (if using).

6. Bake for 15 to 20 minutes, or until the muffins have risen and a metal skewer inserted in the center comes out clean and dry. Remove from the oven and allow to cool in the pan for 2 minutes before turning out onto a wire rack to cool completely.

Notes:

- You can use any vegetables you like for these little savory muffins, such as carrot, broccoli, spinach, or tomato.

- Store the egg muffins in an airtight container in the fridge for 2 days.

- These make fantastic lunch box fillers and are great for picnics too!

FISH FINGERS

Fish fingers have been a staple in Pete's daughters' lives since they were tiny tots, and they're still a favorite now. These little gems are delicious with just a squeeze of fresh lemon juice.

SERVES 4

Prep time: 15 minutes   **Cook time:** 5–7 minutes   **Allergens:** egg, nuts, fish

1 cup (110 g) tapioca flour or arrowroot

3 free-range, organic eggs, lightly whisked

2 cups (200 g) almond meal

2 tablespoons finely chopped parsley

1⅓ pounds (600 g) fish fillets (try flathead, whiting, or snapper), skinned, pin-boned, and cut into finger-size pieces

1 cup (240 ml) cold-pressed, virgin coconut oil

Lemon wedges, to serve

Aïoli (page 239), *optional*, to serve

1. Place the tapioca flour in a shallow bowl and the eggs in a second bowl. Mix the almond meal and parsley together in a third bowl. Dip each fillet in the flour, shaking off the excess. Next, coat it in the egg, then roll in the almond crumbs, patting down firmly.

2. Melt the coconut oil in a frying pan over high heat. When hot enough (the oil should sizzle when the fish is added), shallow-fry the fish in batches for 60 seconds on each side or until golden and crispy.

3. Drain the fish fillets on paper towel. Serve with fresh lemon wedges and aïoli.

PORK AND CABBAGE DUMPLINGS

I love this simple little dumpling recipe. It is not only great for the little ones, but also for the rest of the family, and can become a fun task that everyone helps out with. If you like yours a little spicy, add some chopped chili pepper on the side (adults only!).

SERVES 4–6 (20–22 DUMPLINGS)

Prep time: 30 minutes   **Cook time:** 5 minutes   **Allergens:** soy, egg, sesame

2 cups (150 g) finely chopped cabbage
12 oz (350 g) free-range ground pork
1 free-range, organic egg
½ scallion, finely chopped
1 clove garlic, finely chopped
½ teaspoon finely grated ginger
1 teaspoon sesame oil
1 teaspoon tamari
¼ teaspoon five-spice powder
¼ teaspoon freshly ground black pepper
Chopped cilantro, to serve

BROTH
3 cups (750 ml) chicken broth (page 33)
1 small carrot, peeled and finely diced

1. Place the cabbage in a bowl. Allow the cabbage to sit for 10 to 15 minutes to draw out its liquid. Squeeze the cabbage with your hands to remove as much liquid as possible and transfer to another bowl. Add the remaining ingredients (except the cilantro) to the cabbage and mix well to combine. Roll the meat mixture into bite-size balls approximately ¾ inch (2 cm) in diameter.

2. Bring a large pot of water to a boil over a high heat. Reduce the heat to a simmer. Cook the balls in batches for 3 or 4 minutes, occasionally stirring with a wooden spoon so they don't stick to the bottom of the pot. They will float to the surface when they are cooked through. Drain and set aside.

3. Meanwhile, bring the chicken broth to a boil over medium heat. Add the carrot, reduce the heat, and simmer for 5 minutes or until the carrot is soft.

4. To serve, place the cooked dumplings in bowls and ladle over the broth. Finish with a sprinkle of chopped cilantro.

STICKY PORK BALLS

Tell me a little person who doesn't love a meatball . . . or a big person, for that matter. This recipe is a great way to sneak those veggies in. It can all be blended together, and the only time spent is in browning the meatballs and reducing the sauce.

SERVES 4–6 (~35 MINI MEATBALLS)

Prep time: 20 minutes   **Cook time:** 15 minutes   **Allergens:** egg, soy (if using tamari)

1 carrot, coarsely chopped
1 zucchini, coarsely chopped
½ apple, coarsely chopped
2 cloves garlic, coarsely chopped
1 pound (480 g) free-range ground
    pork
¾ inch (5 mm) piece of ginger, grated
2 tablespoons coconut aminos or
    tamari
1 free-range, organic egg
Freshly ground black pepper
1 tablespoon cold-pressed, virgin
    coconut oil

VEGGIE SPAGHETTI
2 carrots
2 zucchinis

STICKY SAUCE
1 cup (240 ml) chicken or beef broth
    (page 33 and page 146)
3 tablespoons coconut aminos or
    tamari

1. Place the carrot, zucchini, apple, and garlic in a food processor and process until finely chopped. (If you have a small food processor, just blend it in small batches.)

2. Place the vegetable mixture, ground pork, ginger, coconut aminos or tamari, and egg in a large bowl. Season with pepper and mix well.

3. Roll the mixture into walnut-size balls.

4. Heat the coconut oil in a large frying pan over medium heat. Cook the meatballs in batches for about 6 minutes, rolling them around to brown them on all sides. Drain on paper towels.

5. To make the sauce, heat the broth and coconut aminos or tamari in a large pan over medium heat. Add the meatballs and simmer until the sauce has reduced a little.

6. Meanwhile, slice the carrot and zucchini into spaghetti strips using a mandolin or spiralizer. To serve, divide the veggie spaghetti between serving bowls and top with meatballs and a dollop of sauce.

Notes:

- You can also serve this dish as a dumpling soup with some cilantro on top (just double the quantities for the sauce).

- Alternatively, you can reduce the sauce right down so that it's sticky and gooey—ready for some finger-licking fun.

SHRIMP CAKES IN LETTUCE CUPS

This is a fun and simple recipe that kids love helping to prepare—and eat.

SERVES 5

Prep time: 15–20 minutes   **Cook time:** 5 minutes   **Allergens:** shellfish, fish, sesame

1 pound (450 g) raw jumbo shrimp (king prawns), shelled, deveined, and chopped
1 teaspoon fish sauce
1 clove garlic, finely chopped
1 tablespoon finely chopped red pepper
½ scallion, finely chopped
1 teaspoon ice-cold water
1 teaspoon sesame seeds
1–2 tablespoons cold-pressed, virgin coconut oil, melted
Freshly ground black pepper
Juice of ½ lime, *optional*
1 Persian cucumber, sliced
½ avocado, pitted and sliced
5 cherry tomatoes, halved
½ iceberg lettuce, inner leaves separated into 5 little lettuce cups

1. Process the shrimp in a food processor until smooth and sticky. Add the fish sauce, garlic, red pepper, and scallion and pulse until just combined. Add 1 teaspoon of ice-cold filtered water, then pulse to form a thick, coarse paste.

2. Rub your palms with a few drops of coconut oil so the prawn mixture won't stick to them. Divide the mixture into 5 equal portions and shape them into patties. Place the sesame seeds in a small bowl and roll the shrimp cakes in them to coat.

3. Preheat a barbecue or chargrill pan on high and brush with the coconut oil. Cook the shrimp cakes for 5 minutes, turning occasionally, until golden and cooked through.

4. Sprinkle with a little pepper, then drizzle with the lime juice (if using).

5. To serve, place a lettuce cup on each plate, then pop the patties, cucumber, avocado, and cherry tomatoes in separate bowls, and let the children assemble the cups themselves.

BEST BOLOGNESE SAUCE

SERVES 10

Prep time: 15 minutes   **Cook time:** 3–4 hours   **Allergens:** none

3 tablespoons cold-pressed, virgin coconut oil

2 onions, chopped

3 cloves garlic, finely chopped

2 teaspoons smoked paprika

4 celery stalks, finely chopped

2 carrots, finely chopped

2¼ pounds (1 k) grass-fed ground beef

¼ cauliflower (about 7 oz/200 g), finely chopped

¼ broccoli (about 4 oz/120 g), finely chopped

1 zucchini, finely chopped

2 cups (100 g) finely chopped kale

4 tomatoes, chopped

2 tablespoons chopped basil leaves

1 tablespoon dried oregano

1 cup (240 ml) chicken or beef broth (page 33 and 146), plus extra if needed

3 cups (700 ml) tomato puree, plus extra if needed

TO SERVE

Dulse flakes

Basil and parsley leaves

1. Place the coconut oil in a large pot over medium-high heat. Add the onion and sauté until soft and translucent (about 5 minutes). Add the garlic and paprika and cook until fragrant (about 30 seconds), stirring constantly. Next, add the celery and carrot and cook for a further 5 minutes or until slightly browned and softened.

2. Add the ground beef and brown for 5 or 6 minutes, breaking up the meat with a wooden spoon. Add the cauliflower, broccoli, zucchini, kale, tomatoes, basil, oregano, broth, and puree, and stir to combine. Cover, reduce heat, and gently simmer, stirring occasionally, for 3 hours until all the vegetables are soft and tender (you can also use a slow cooker). Check occasionally to make sure it doesn't need any extra broth or puree.

3. Before serving, stir in a tablespoon of dulse flakes. Divide between bowls and top each with fresh basil and parsley leaves.

Note:

*   This is the perfect meal for little fusspots. It's a wonderful way to pack in loads of nutrition with every mouthful. Use any vegetables you can find in the fridge. Blend them up so even the pickiest detective can't see them.

ASIAN MEATBALLS WITH MAYO

SERVES 4–6

Prep time: 15 minutes   **Cook time:** 15–20 minutes   **Allergens:** sesame, soy (if using)

10½ ounces (300 g) ground grass-fed beef

10½ ounces (300 g) ground free-range pork

4½ ounces (130 g) field mushrooms, finely chopped

1 small carrot, finely chopped

2 free-range egg yolks

1 small onion, finely chopped

1 tablespoon fish sauce

1 tablespoon sesame oil

1 tablespoon tomato paste

1 tablespoon coconut aminos or tamari

2 cloves garlic, finely chopped

½ teaspoon ground cumin

½ teaspoon ground coriander

½ teaspoon freshly ground black pepper

TO SERVE

Mayonnaise (page 238) or Aïoli (page 239), *optional*

Black and white sesame seeds

1. Preheat the oven to 350°F (180°C). Line a large baking sheet with parchment paper. Place all the ingredients in a large bowl and mix well with a wooden spoon.

2. Roll the mixture into walnut-size balls and place them on the lined baking sheet in a single layer, making sure they are not touching each other.

3. Bake the meatballs for 15 to 20 minutes or until cooked through. Remove from the oven and allow to cool slightly before serving.

4. Serve with homemade mayo or Aïoli and a sprinkle of sesame seeds.

SOFT-BOILED EGGS WITH SALMON ROE

SERVES 3–6

Prep time: 5 minutes   **Cook time:** 5 minutes   **Allergens:** fish, egg

6 free-range, organic eggs
1½ tablespoons salmon roe
Dulse flakes, to serve

1. Place the eggs in a large saucepan and cover them completely with cold water. Bring to a boil over high heat and cook to your liking (4 or 5 minutes for soft yolks, 7 minutes for hard yolks).

2. Cut the tops off the eggs and place the eggs in egg cups. Spoon 1 teaspoon of salmon roe on top of each egg and finish with a sprinkle of dulse flakes before serving. Don't forget to eat the egg tops, too!

ZOODLE BOLOGNESE

This is a fabulous way to pack in nutrient-dense food and loads of veggies in a fun, colorful and playful manner. I guarantee your kids will love it.

SERVES 4–6

Prep time: 5–10 minutes   **Cook time:** 2 minutes   **Allergens:** none

1 tablespoon cold-pressed, virgin coconut oil or other good-quality fat
2 zucchinis, sliced into spaghetti strips using a mandolin or spiralizer
2 carrots, sliced into spaghetti strips using a mandolin or spiralizer
Best Bolognese Sauce (page 65), to serve

1. To make the zoodles, heat the oil in a frying pan over medium-high heat.

2. Add the zucchini and carrot and sauté for 1 to 1½ minutes, or until just beginning to soften. Spoon into bowls and top with a good spoonful of Bolognese. Serve.

HOT DOG WITH A SWEET POTATO BUN

Looking at this image, I immediately think it is a regular hot dog with a bun. In fact, I have replaced the bun with a slow-roasted sweet potato and topped it with a delicious gourmet wheat-free sausage that you can make yourself or pick up from a quality butcher or health food store. These are super easy to make and will be a hit at your next kids' party. I like to serve some kraut or a little garden salad on the side.

SERVES 2

Prep time: 10 minutes   **Cook time:** 6 hours   **Allergens:** sesame seeds

2 sweet potatoes, unpeeled (try to pick out straight ones if possible)

1½ teaspoons sesame seeds

1 tablespoon coconut oil or other good-quality fat

2 gourmet sausages of your choice

Tomato Ketchup (see page 241), to serve

Dijon mustard, to serve

1. Preheat the oven to 225°F (110°C).

2. Place the sweet potatoes on a baking pan and roast for about 6 hours, or until very tender. Cut the sweet potatoes almost in half lengthwise. Do not cut all the way through. Slightly open up the cut center part, then carefully peel away the skin, sprinkle with the sesame seeds, and set aside.

3. Meanwhile, heat the oil or fat in a large frying pan over medium-high heat. Add the sausages and reduce the heat to medium. Cook, turning occasionally, for 8 to 10 minutes, or until cooked through.

4. Place the sausages lengthwise in the center cut part of the sweet potato. Squeeze over some ketchup and mustard and serve.

MEATZZA

I recently added this meat-based pizza to the menu at a restaurant I am consulting for in Canada, and it has become the owner's favorite. I simply replaced the traditional dough with a burger patty pressed out to resemble a pizza base and, I have to say, it is delicious. Add your favorite pizza toppings, such as olives, anchovies, tomato, fresh or dried herbs and, of course, more meat, such as pepperoni or ham. It is up to you what type of cheese you put on top, but I use a nondairy one as it works better for my body. Kids love this meatzza—and it is so good for them in so many ways.

SERVES 2–3

Prep time: 25 minutes **Cook time:** 18 minutes **Allergens:** egg

BASE

7 ounces (200 g) ground beef
7 ounces (200 g) ground pork
1 egg yolk
¼ onion, finely diced
1 clove garlic, finely chopped
1 tablespoon finely chopped flat-leaf parsley leaves
½ teaspoon dried oregano
¾ teaspoon sea salt
¼ teaspoon freshly ground black pepper

TOPPINGS

Coconut oil, for greasing
⅓ cup (80 ml) Pizza Sauce (page 76)
6 basil leaves, coarsely torn, plus extra leaves to serve
1 Roma tomato, finely sliced
½ cup (80 g) vegan mozzarella, torn into small pieces
Sea salt and freshly ground black pepper

1. Preheat the oven to 475°F (245°C) or the highest temperature setting. Grease a 12-inch (30½-cm) pizza pan with a little coconut oil and line with parchment paper. Place all the base ingredients in a bowl and mix until well combined.

2. Transfer the base mixture to the prepared pizza pan and, using your hands, press it out to evenly cover the surface. Bake for 6 to 8 minutes until the meat is cooked through. Remove and drain any liquid from the pan.

3. Spread the pizza sauce evenly over the base. Scatter the torn basil leaves on top, then arrange the tomato slices and vegan mozzarella. Season with a little salt and pepper.

4. Return the meatzza to the oven and bake for a further 5 to 10 minutes until lightly browned. Use the paper to carefully transfer the meatzza to a chopping board or plate. Cut into slices, scatter over the extra basil leaves, and serve.

MARGHERITA PIZZA

Tomato and basil have got to be among the greatest flavor combinations of all time. Just ask the Italians, who use them in so many dishes, including caprese salad, spaghetti and meatballs, and the most famous of all—the Margherita pizza (named in honor of Queen Margherita in 1889 by a local Italian pizza maker). Here, I have replaced the buffalo mozzarella with cashew cheese to make it dairy free, but the rest is the same—tomato, basil, and a crispy base to carry these amazing flavors.

SERVES 4

Prep time: 20 minutes   **Cook time:** 15 minutes   **Allergens:** nuts, eggs

PALEO PIZZA BASE
2½ cups (260 g) almond meal
1 cup (130 g) arrowroot or tapioca flour
1½ teaspoons baking powder
1 teaspoon sea salt
3 eggs
4 tablespoons macadamia oil or melted coconut oil
½ cup (120 ml) nut milk

TOPPINGS
2 tablespoons chopped flat-leaf parsley leaves
6 cherry tomatoes, sliced
½ cup (120 g) Cashew Cheese (page 242)
Sea salt and freshly ground black pepper
8 basil leaves, to serve
2 macadamia nuts, grated, to serve
Extra-virgin olive oil, to serve

PIZZA SAUCE
1 (14-oz/400 g) can whole peeled tomatoes
¼ teaspoon Himalayan salt or sea salt
1 teaspoon dried oregano
2 pinches of freshly ground black pepper

1. To make the paleo pizza base, preheat the oven to 350°F (180°C). Line a large baking sheet with parchment paper.

2. Combine the almond meal, arrowroot or tapioca flour, baking powder, and salt in a large bowl. In a separate bowl, whisk together the eggs, oil, and nut milk.

3. Fold the egg mixture into the dry ingredients, one-third at a time, and mix thoroughly to form a smooth, thick dough.

4. Spoon the dough onto the prepared baking sheet. Using a palette knife or spatula, spread the dough out in a round or rectangular shape to a thickness of ¼ inch (5 mm). You can make the pizza bases as big or small as you like depending on who it is for (kids usually love to have their own individual pizzas!). This amount of dough will make two 12-inch (30½-cm) round pizza bases. Bake for 5 minutes until the pizza base is cooked through and lightly browned.

5. Remove from the oven and set aside to cool.

6. To make the pizza sauce, combine all the ingredients in a food processor and process until smooth.

7. Increase the oven to 475°F (240°C) or as high as it will go.

8. Flip the pizza base and evenly spread over 4 tablespoons of pizza sauce. Scatter on the parsley and cherry tomato slices and dollop the cashew cheese on top. Season with salt and pepper. Return to the oven and cook for a further 5 to 10 minutes, or until golden and crisp. Remove from the oven, cut into portions, and garnish with the basil leaves, grated macadamia nuts, and a drizzle of olive oil.

9. Leftover pizza sauce can be stored in an airtight container in the fridge for up to 1 week or in the freezer for up to 3 months.

FISH TACOS WITH CELERIAC RÉMOULADE

SERVES 4

Prep time: 30 minutes   **Cook time:** 6 minutes   **Allergens:** egg, fish, nuts

1¼ pounds (550 g) flathead fillets (or any firm whitefish such as whiting, snapper or Spanish mackerel), skinned and pin-boned
½ cup (2 oz/60 g) tapioca flour
2 free-range organic eggs, lightly beaten with 3 tablespoons water
1 cup (3½ oz/100 g) almond meal or 1 cup (2 oz /60 g) dried coconut
Coconut oil for deep-frying
8 butter lettuce leaves
Lemon halves, to serve

CELERIAC RÉMOULADE

8½ ounces (240 g) celeriac, peeled
2 red radishes, julienned
½ cup (125 ml) Aïoli (page 239)
1 tablespoon finely chopped chervil leaves
1 tablespoon finely chopped flat-leaf parsley leaves
Juice and zest of 1 lemon
Himalayan salt or sea salt
Freshly ground black pepper

1. To make the celeriac rémoulade, grate the celeriac or julienne it using a mandolin. Celeriac tends to discolor quickly, so place it in cold water with a little bit of lemon juice. Combine the radish, aïoli, chervil, parsley, and lemon juice in a bowl and season to taste. Drain the celeriac, pat dry on paper towels, and stir it into the aïoli mixture.

2. Taste for seasoning and transfer to a small bowl.

3. To make the guacamole, combine all the ingredients in a small bowl. Set aside.

4. Cut the flathead fillets into eight even portions. Place the tapioca flour in a shallow bowl, the egg mixture in another shallow bowl, and the almond meal or coconut in a third bowl. Season the fish with a little salt, dust lightly with tapioca flour, dip the fish pieces in the egg mixture and coat with the almond meal or coconut, pressing them firmly.

5. Heat the coconut oil to 325°F (160°C) in a wok or large saucepan.

6. To test the temperature, drop a small piece of fish in the oil—it should bubble instantly around the edges. Working in batches, fry the fish for 90 seconds until cooked through. Drain on paper towels and season with salt.

7. Place the lettuce leaves, rémoulade, guacamole, fish, and lemon wedges on a serving platter for everyone to serve themselves. To assemble your lettuce cup "tacos," fill each lettuce leaf with some rémoulade, then guacamole and a piece of fish.

8. Squeeze the lemon juice over the top.

GUACAMOLE

1 avocado, diced

1 small red chili, deseeded and finely diced, *optional*

¼ red bell pepper, finely diced

Juice of 1 lime

1–2 tablespoons finely diced red onion

1 clove garlic, finely chopped

2 tablespoons chopped cilantro leaves

1 tablespoon extra-virgin olive oil

CHICKEN NOODLE SOUP

There are healing properties in a bowl of chicken soup that people have known about for centuries. Chicken and other bone broths are especially soothing if you have any sort of digestive problem. These broths contain numerous minerals that are easily assimilated by the body: calcium, magnesium, phosphorous, silicon, and many other trace minerals and amino acids. They also provide chondroitin sulphates and glucosamine that help with arthritis and joint pain. And we cannot forget about gelatin, the ingredient in broths that strengthens the gut wall, reduces inflammation, and helps with so many illnesses. It is essential to make the stock yourself for this soup.

SERVES 4

Prep time: 20 minutes **Cook time:** 35 minutes **Allergens:** none

2 tablespoons coconut oil or other good-quality fat

1 onion, chopped

3 cloves garlic, crushed

2 carrots, chopped

2 celery stalks, halved lengthwise, and cut into 1-cm chunks

4 thyme sprigs

1 bay leaf

1⅓ quarts (5⅓ cups /1.25 l) chicken stock (page 33)

6 ounces (170 g) kelp noodles, coarsely chopped

1½ cups (300 g) finely shredded leftover cooked chicken

Sea salt and freshly ground black pepper

1 handful flat-leaf parsley leaves, finely chopped

1. Heat the oil or fat in a stockpot or large saucepan over medium heat.

2. Add the onion, garlic, carrot, celery, thyme, and bay leaf. Cook, stirring regularly, for about 6 minutes until the vegetables are softened but not browned. Pour in the chicken stock and bring to a boil. Reduce the heat to low and simmer for 20 minutes.

3. Add the noodles to the pan and simmer for 5 minutes until tender. Stir in the chicken and simmer for a few minutes to heat through. Season with salt and pepper and sprinkle with the parsley before serving.

Variations:

You can substitute cauliflower rice (page 105) or zucchini noodles (page 70) for the kelp noodles if you like.

SATAY CHICKEN SKEWERS

Anything on a stick seems to win everyone over at dinnertime. This is another great recipe to get the kids involved. I always have disposable gloves in the kitchen for messy jobs, which makes it a lot easier cleaning up, and if using turmeric or beet, then our hands and fingers aren't stained. I serve these skewers with a raw and utterly delicious peanut-free satay sauce, which you can whip up in a matter of minutes.

SERVES 4

Prep time: 40 minutes   **Cook time:** 8–10 minutes   **Allergens:** nuts, sesame, soy, fish

1¾ pounds (800 g) chicken thigh fillets, cut into 1-inch (2½ cm) cubes
Sea salt and freshly ground black pepper
Cilantro leaves, to serve
Lime wedges, to serve

MARINADE
1½ teaspoons lime zest
1½ tablespoons lime juice
1 tablespoon coconut oil, melted, plus extra for cooking
3 tablespoons tamari
3 tablespoons fish sauce
3 cloves garlic, crushed
1½ tablespoons finely grated ginger
1½ tablespoons ground turmeric
1½ teaspoons ground coriander
1 teaspoon ground cumin
2 teaspoons sea salt

CASHEW SATAY SAUCE
1 cup (150 g) cashews (activated if possible, see page 245)
½ cup (120 g) almond butter
2 tablespoons finely grated ginger
1 long red chili, deseeded and finely chopped
2 tablespoons tamari
1 tablespoon sesame oil
1 tablespoon maple syrup
Sea salt

1. To make the marinade, combine all the ingredients in a large bowl and mix well. Add the chicken and toss until thoroughly coated. Cover and marinate for at least 2 hours, or refrigerate overnight.

2. Soak 8 bamboo skewers in a shallow dish of cold water for at least 30 minutes. Drain. To make the cashew satay sauce, combine the cashews and almond butter in a food processor and pulse until the nuts are well ground. Add the ginger and chili and process until well blended. Add the tamari, sesame oil, and maple syrup and blend well. Gradually pour in 4 tablespoons of water and pulse until the sauce becomes smooth. If the sauce is a little too thick, simply add more water. Transfer to a serving bowl and set aside. Season with a little salt if desired.

3. Preheat a barbecue or chargrill plate to medium-high.

4. Thread the marinated chicken cubes onto the prepared skewers and season with salt and pepper. Grill the skewers, basting with the marinade and turning often, for 8 to 10 minutes until browned and cooked through.

5. Warm the satay dipping sauce, if desired. Scatter the cilantro leaves over the skewers and serve with lime wedges and the satay sauce on the side.

GLAZED CHRISTMAS HAM

If there is one thing that I have learned that remains one of the most powerful philosophies for cooking at home, it would have to be that cooking in bulk and more than you need for just one meal is one of the best ways to ensure that there is always good-quality food on hand at all times. Whether it be cooking a roast, making a soup, or grilling some sausages, we always like to cook extra so we have it on hand to eat the next day or two. This Christmas Ham recipe doesn't need to be cooked only for the holiday either; any time of the year is great, and eating it cold afterward just by itself, or in a salad, or on some gluten-free bread in a sandwich with mayonnaise and pickles, checks the boxes for me and my family.

SERVES 15–20

Prep time: 15 minutes　**Cook time:** 90 minutes　**Allergens:** none

11-pound (5 kg) cooked cold leg of ham
3 large apples of your choice, halved
3 peaches, halved and pitted

GLAZE
¾ cup (260 g) honey
Zest and juice of 1 orange
1½ teaspoons ground yellow mustard seeds
1½ teaspoons ground cinnamon
¼ teaspoon ground cloves
¼ teaspoon freshly grated nutmeg
¼ teaspoon ground allspice

1. Preheat the oven to 320°F (160°C).

2. Prepare the ham by lifting off the skin but leaving the fat. Score a diamond pattern into the fat. (This helps to open the ham up and to allow the flavor to penetrate into the meat.)

3. To make the glaze, combine all the ingredients with 3 tablespoons of water in a bowl and mix well.

4. Spread the glaze over the ham. Place the ham in a roasting pan and pour in water to a depth of 1 inch (2½ cm). Bake for 30 minutes. Remove from the oven and scatter the apples and peaches around the ham. Return to the oven and bake for another 30 to 60 minutes, basting the fruit and ham from time to time. (Be careful not to let the ham burn.) Cover with foil and set aside in a warm place to rest for 15 minutes before slicing.

5. Slice the ham and serve with the spiced fruit.

BUTTER CHICKEN

This is a recipe that has really surprised a lot of parents when they cooked it for the first time for their children, as a lot of people believe that spices can be a bit too much for their little ones. I always encourage parents to start including different spices and herbs into their cooking as we all can learn and train our taste buds to learn to appreciate new and exciting flavors, which leads to a developed palate and exploring new things in life. The feedback I have from parents who cook this recipe for their families is that they absolutely love the flavors in this dish, and that it has become one of their all-time favorite family recipes.

SERVES 4

Prep time: 30 minutes   **Cook time:** 30 minutes   **Allergens:** none

2 tablespoons coconut oil

1 large onion, diced

4 cloves garlic, crushed

2 teaspoons garam masala

1 teaspoon ground cardamom

1 teaspoon ground coriander

1 teaspoon ground ginger

1 teaspoon ground cumin

½ teaspoon paprika

1–2 pinches cayenne pepper, *optional*

1 teaspoon ground turmeric

3 tablespoons tomato paste

1 teaspoon sea salt

2 tablespoons lemon juice

1 (15-oz) can coconut cream

1½ pounds (700 g) chicken thigh fillets, cut into bite-size pieces

Cilantro leaves, to serve

Cauliflower Rice (page 105), to serve

1. Heat the coconut oil in a large saucepan over medium heat.

2. Add the onion and sauté for 4 minutes until translucent. Turn the heat down to low and stir in the garlic and spices. Add the tomato paste and cook for 1 minute. Add the salt, lemon juice, and coconut cream and mix well.

3. Turn the heat up to medium and bring the sauce to a simmer. Add the chicken and stir until well coated with the sauce. Cover the pan with a lid and cook, stirring occasionally, for 20 to 25 minutes, or until the chicken is cooked through and the sauce has thickened.

4. Garnish with the cilantro and serve with the cauliflower rice.

ROAST CHICKEN
WITH ROSEMARY, GARLIC, AND LEMON

Rosemary, garlic, and lemon. Whenever I think about these three ingredients, all I see is roast chicken in all its glory. The purpose of this book is to offer real-life solutions to time-poor families who value their health, and this recipe fits the bill perfectly. It takes very little time and uses just a few quality ingredients that most families will have on hand. I have chosen whole chicken legs here as they are quicker to cook than a whole bird. For an even quicker meal, use wings. Serve with a big bowl of roasted veggies or a salad.

SERVES 4

Prep time: 25 minutes (plus 2 hours or overnight marinating)
Cook time: 35–45 minutes   **Allergens:** none

⅓ cup (80 g) coconut oil or other good-quality fat, melted

2 tablespoons honey, *optional*

1 teaspoon paprika

1 teaspoon onion powder

1 tablespoon Italian seasoning

¼ teaspoon dried chili flakes

sea salt and freshly ground black pepper

4 whole chicken legs (thigh and drumstick) (about 2½ lb/1.2 kg in total)

2 lemons, quartered

1 bulb garlic, halved across the cloves

4 French shallots, peeled and halved

1 teaspoon dried oregano

3 rosemary sprigs, torn into pieces

Chopped herbs (such as rosemary, thyme, and flat-leaf parsley), to serve

1. In a small bowl, whisk together the oil or fat, honey (if using), paprika, onion powder, Italian seasoning, chili flakes, and salt and pepper.

2. Place the chicken in a roasting pan and spread out the pieces so they cook evenly. Pour the oil mixture over the chicken, turning to coat on all sides. Arrange the lemon, garlic, and shallot around and under the chicken and sprinkle on the herbs. For best results, cover the chicken and place in the fridge to marinate for at least 2 hours or overnight.

3. Preheat the oven to 375°F (190°C).

4. Season the chicken with salt and pepper and roast for 35 to 45 minutes, or until the chicken is cooked through, the skin is crispy, and the juices run clear when pierced with the tip of a knife. (Remove the garlic if it's starting to darken too quickly and return to the pan 2 minutes before the chicken is ready.) Garnish with the chopped herbs and serve with roasted vegetables. Squeeze over the roasted lemon wedges at the table.

BACON AND EGG FAT BOMBS

One of the most common questions I get asked is what to feed hungry teenagers. This recipe really comes in handy and will keep teenagers—as well as the rest of the family—happy and full between meals. It's a great idea to whip up a big batch of these on the weekend so you can direct the family to the fridge to get their fat fix throughout the week, and you can feel good knowing they'll be satiated until mealtime. These make great lunch box additions alongside some fresh or cooked vegetables and sauerkraut.

MAKES 10

Prep time: 10 minutes (plus 1 hour chilling and setting time)
Cook time: 15–20 minutes   **Allergens:** egg

6 slices bacon
4 large hard-boiled eggs, peeled
4 tablespoons coconut oil or good-quality animal fat, melted
4 tablespoons mayonnaise
1½ tablespoons chopped flat-leaf parsley leaves
Sea salt and freshly ground black pepper
Veggie sticks, to serve, *optional*

1. Preheat the oven to 400°F (200°C). Grease and line a baking sheet with parchment paper. Arrange the bacon on the prepared baking sheet in a single layer, making sure the strips are not touching. Bake, turning the baking sheet once for even cooking, for 15 to 20 minutes until the bacon is golden and crisp. Keep a close eye on the bacon to prevent it from burning. Set aside until needed and reserve the bacon fat for the egg mixture.

2. Mash the eggs in a bowl, then add the oil or fat, the reserved bacon fat, the mayonnaise, and the parsley. Mix gently until combined. Season with salt and pepper. Cover with plastic wrap and refrigerate for 30 minutes.

3. Meanwhile, chop the bacon into small pieces ready for rolling.

4. Remove the egg mixture from the fridge and roll into ten walnut-size balls. Roll each ball in the bacon bits to coat, then place on a baking sheet and refrigerate for 20 to 30 minutes until slightly firm. Enjoy the fat bombs on their own or serve with a side of veggie sticks, if desired.

ROSEMARY SEED CRACKERS WITH CHICKEN AND MAYONNAISE SALAD

When we cook a glorious roast chicken at home, we generally eat about half of it and then enjoy the other half as leftovers for days to come. We use the leftovers in soups, salads, and omelets, or make a yummy chicken and mayonnaise salad like this, which is just perfect between slices of paleo bread or dolloped on seed crackers.

SERVES 4

Prep time: 35 minutes   **Cook time:** 25–30 minutes   **Allergens:** egg

ROSEMARY SEED CRACKERS
¼ cup (30 g) sunflower seeds
½ cup (75 g) pumpkin seeds
1½ tablespoons freshly ground flaxseeds
2 teaspoons psyllium husks
2 teaspoons finely chopped rosemary
¼ teaspoon fine sea salt
3 tablespoons filtered water
1½ tablespoons coconut oil or good-quality animal fat, melted
1 egg
Tapioca flour, for dusting
Olive oil, for brushing
Flaky sea salt, for sprinkling

AVOCADO PUREE
1 avocado, seed removed
1 tablespoon lemon juice

CHICKEN AND MAYONNAISE SALAD
7 ounces (200 g) cooked chicken, shredded
⅓ cup (90 g) Mayonnaise (page 238)
1 teaspoon lemon juice

1. Preheat the oven to 350°F (180°C).

2. To make the crackers, combine the sunflower seeds, pumpkin seeds, flaxseed, psyllium husks, rosemary, and salt in the bowl of a food processor and process to a fine powder. Add the water, the coconut oil or fat, and the egg and continue processing until the dough comes together to form a slightly wet and sticky paste. Transfer the dough to a work surface dusted with tapioca flour. Roll into a ball, place on a large sheet of parchment paper, and pat down to flatten into a disc. Allow to rest for 10 minutes. Place another large sheet of parchment paper over the flattened dough and, using a rolling pin, roll out to a thickness of ⅛ inch (2 mm). Peel away the top sheet of paper and discard. Using a pizza cutter or sharp knife, cut into rectangles or your desired shape and size. Transfer the dough shapes and the parchment paper to a baking sheet. Brush the shapes with a light coating of olive oil and sprinkle with the flaky salt. Bake, turning the baking sheet halfway through, for 25 to 30 minutes until golden. Allow to cool completely before removing from the baking sheet and serving. Store in an airtight container in the pantry for up to 1 week.

3. To make the avocado puree, place the avocado and lemon juice in the bowl of a food processor and

1 teaspoon chopped tarragon leaves

1 teaspoon finely chopped curly or flat-leaf parsley leaves

Sea salt and freshly ground black pepper

TO SERVE

1 baby romaine lettuce, finely shredded

2 radishes, cut into matchsticks

1 small handful chervil sprigs

Extra-virgin olive oil

blend until smooth and creamy. Season with salt and pepper. Transfer to a bowl and set aside until needed.

4. To make the chicken and mayonnaise salad, place the chicken, mayonnaise, lemon juice, and chopped herbs in a bowl and mix well to combine. Season with salt and pepper.

5. Place the rosemary seed crackers on a platter and top each with some lettuce, then dollop on a tablespoon of avocado puree and a spoonful of chicken and mayo salad. Scatter on the radish and chervil, drizzle on some extra-virgin olive oil, and serve.

CAULIFLOWER AND BACON TOAST

These fun little cauliflower toasts make a welcome addition to lunch boxes. They are delicious cold or hot. Make a big batch and serve with fried eggs and greens, or top with bacon, or place under some grilled salmon or steak and add a dollop of delicious aïoli.

SERVES 4

Prep time: 10 minutes   **Cook time:** 25 minutes   **Allergens:** egg

¼ head of cauliflower
   (about 12⅓ oz/350 g), chopped
   into small pieces
2½ tablespoons coconut oil
Sea salt and freshly ground black pepper
2 slices bacon (about 4¼ oz/120 g),
   finely diced
2 eggs

TO SERVE
Lemon wedges
Fried eggs
Sliced avocado

1. Preheat the oven to 350°F (180°C). Line a large baking sheet with parchment paper. Place the cauliflower in the bowl of a food processor and process to fine crumbs.

2. Melt 1 tablespoon of the coconut oil in a large frying pan over medium heat. Add the cauliflower crumbs and cook for 4 to 6 minutes until softened. Season with salt and pepper, transfer to a large bowl, and allow to cool.

3. Wipe the pan clean, add 2 teaspoons of the oil, and fry the bacon over medium-high heat for 3 or 4 minutes until lightly golden. Allow to cool.

4. Add the cooled bacon to the cauliflower, add the eggs, and mix to combine. Season with salt and pepper. Spoon 2 tablespoons of the cauliflower mixture onto the prepared sheet and gently spread out to form a patty approximately 3 inches (8 cm) in diameter. Repeat, allowing 1 inch (2½ cm) space between each patty, until all the mixture is used and you have four patties in total. Bake for 10 minutes, or until firm. Allow to cool.

5. Heat the remaining oil in a frying pan over medium-high heat. Cook the patties for 1–1½ minutes on each side until golden. Serve immediately with some lemon wedges, fried eggs, and avocado.

SALAMI AND OLIVE EGG MUFFINS

There is a lot of talk about whether processed meats such as ham, salami, and bacon are indeed healthy foods. My take on it is, if the pigs are healthy and have been fed a wholesome diet and raised in good conditions, and the curing process has been done in a traditional way (using good-quality salt), then, yes, by all means, include some processed meat in your diet. If you don't have access to top-quality salami for this recipe, use roast chicken or pork or go vegetarian.

MAKES 12

Prep time: 10 minutes   **Cook time:** 15 minutes   **Allergens:** egg

10 eggs
Sea salt and freshly ground black
    pepper
12 large slices of salami
24 pitted kalamata olives or olives of
    your choice
24 semi-dried tomatoes (see recipe
    below)
24 basil leaves, torn

1. Preheat the oven to 350°F (180°C). Grease a 12-hole standard muffin tin.

2. Crack the eggs into a large bowl and lightly whisk. Season with salt and pepper. Line each muffin hole with a slice of salami, covering the base and side completely.

3. Evenly divide the olives, semi-dried tomatoes, and basil among the holes, then spoon in the egg mixture until level with the rim. Bake for 15 minutes, or until the muffins have risen and a skewer inserted in the center of a muffin comes out clean and dry. Allow the muffins to cool in the pan for two minutes before turning out. Serve the muffins while still warm or chill and use for school lunches. Store in an airtight container in the fridge for up to two days.

SEMI-DRIED TOMATOES

MAKES 2 CUPS

Prep time: 5 minutes   **Cook time:** 1½ hours   **Allergens:** none

1 pound (450 g) cherry tomatoes, halved

Sea salt and freshly ground black pepper

1½ teaspoons dried oregano

½ cup (100 ml) extra-virgin olive oil

1. Preheat the oven to 250°F (120°C). Line a baking sheet with parchment paper and place a wire rack on the baking sheet.

2. Arrange the cherry tomatoes, cut-side up, on the wire rack. Season the tomatoes with salt and pepper and sprinkle on the dried oregano. Bake in the oven for 1½ hours, or until the tomatoes are dry around the edges but still soft in the center. Set aside to cool completely. Transfer the tomatoes to a sterilized glass jar, pour in the olive oil, seal and store in the fridge for up to 2 weeks.

FISH MUFFINS

Monica and her twin sister, Jacinta, are brilliant chefs and dear friends, who have been working along-side me for the last twelve years. I trust them with my life and the lives of my children. From time to time the girls look after my daughters and have them for sleepovers. On these occasions, Monica and Jacinta make their famous fish muffins, which go down a treat! I always ask for a batch so we can pack them into lunch boxes during the week.

Thanks ladies, I am forever indebted to you both, xo.

MAKES 12

Prep time: 20 minutes   **Cook time:** 25 minutes   **Allergens:** egg, fish

1 large zucchini (about 8½ oz/240 g), grated

2 carrots (about 7 oz/200 g), grated

1½ teaspoons fine sea salt

Coconut oil or good-quality animal fat, for greasing

4 eggs, beaten

¼ teaspoon baking soda

10 ounces (280 g) tuna, salmon, mackerel, or sardines in brine or spring water, drained

2 tablespoons chopped curly or flat-leaf parsley leaves

2 teaspoons coconut flour

Zest of ½ lemon

Freshly ground black pepper

QUICK TARTAR SAUCE
¾ cup (185 g) Mayonnaise (page 238)

1 tablespoon salted capers, rinsed well, patted dry and chopped

TO SERVE
Lemon wedges

1 head baby romaine lettuce, leaves separated

1. Combine the zucchini and carrot in a colander. Sprinkle with the salt and mix through. Leave the vegetables to release moisture for 15 minutes, then squeeze out all the liquid from the zucchini and carrot with your hands.

2. You can also wrap the vegetables in a clean dish towel and squeeze the liquid out that way. Preheat the oven to 400°F (200°C).

3. Grease a 12-hole standard muffin pan with oil or fat.

4. Place the eggs and baking soda in a large bowl and whisk to combine. Add the zucchini and carrot, fish, parsley, coconut flour, and lemon zest and season with some pepper. Mix until well incorporated. Spoon the mixture evenly into the holes of the prepared muffin tin.

5. Bake for 25 minutes, or until the muffins are firm and cooked through. Allow the muffins to cool in the pan for 2 minutes before turning out onto a wire rack to cool completely.

6. Meanwhile, to make the quick tartar sauce, place the mayonnaise and capers in a small bowl and mix to combine.

7. Set aside until needed.

8. Serve the muffins with some tartar sauce and the lemon wedges and lettuce leaves on the side.

GREEK-STYLE LAMB MUFFINS

Growing up, I remember having mint jelly on my roast lamb–with this delicious lunch box treat I hope to re-create that memory for schoolkids everywhere.

MAKES 12

Prep time: 15–20 minutes   **Cook time:** 15–20 minutes   **Allergens:** egg

⅓ cup (80 ml) coconut oil or good-quality animal fat, plus extra for greasing
1 red onion, finely chopped
3 cloves garlic, finely chopped
1 teaspoon ground cumin
¼ teaspoon chili flakes, *optional*
1⅓ pounds (600 g) ground lamb
1 tablespoon dried mint
2 tablespoons dried oregano
2 eggs, lightly beaten
Sea salt and freshly ground black pepper

TO SERVE
Salad of your choice
Mint Jelly (see recipe below)

1. Preheat the oven to 350°F (180°C) and lightly grease a 12-hole standard muffin pan with a little oil or fat.

2. Heat the oil or fat in a frying pan over medium heat. Add the onion and sauté for about 5 minutes until softened and translucent. Add the garlic and cook for a further minute, then add the cumin and chili flakes (if using) and cook for 30 seconds, or until fragrant. Set aside.

3. In a large bowl, mix the ground lamb with the cooked onion mixture, dried herbs, eggs, and some salt and pepper until well incorporated. Spoon the mixture evenly into the holes of the prepared pan, then bake for 15 to 20 minutes until the muffins are cooked through. Cool slightly for 1 minute. The muffins may release a little bit of liquid, so drain well before you turn them out of the tin. Serve the muffins with a salad of your choice and some mint jelly on the side.

. . . .

MINT JELLY

MAKES 2½ CUPS (600 G)

Prep time: 8 minutes (plus 4 hours to set)   **Cook time:** 10 minutes   **Allergens:** none

2 Granny Smith apples, cored and chopped but not peeled
2 cups filtered water
1 tablespoon lemon juice
2 large handfuls mint leaves, *divided*
1½ tablespoons powdered gelatin
3 tablespoons honey, or to taste

1. Place the apple, 2 cups of filtered water, the lemon juice, and 1 handful of mint leaves in a saucepan and bring to a simmer. Cook for 10 minutes until the apple is soft. Remove from the heat, add the gelatin and honey, and stir until the gelatin dissolves. Allow to cool completely. Place the apple mixture in the bowl of a food processor and blend until smooth. Pass through a fine sieve and discard the leftover pulp.

2. Finely chop the remaining mint and mix into the apple mixture. Pour into a glass jar, cover, and refrigerate for 4 hours, or until set to a wobbly jelly consistency. Give it a good mix before serving.

SUPER-SIMPLE MEATY MUFFINS

There is nothing remotely hard about this recipe, and there is no reason you can't cook up a big batch of meaty muffins on Sunday, enjoy them for lunch or dinner, then use the leftover muffins for lunches for the first couple of days of the school week. Simply presented in the lunch box with some fresh salad, a low-sugar tomato ketchup, and some gherkins or olives, they'll go down an absolute treat.

MAKES 12

Prep time: 20 minutes   **Cook time:** 22 minutes   **Allergens:** egg, soy

1 tablespoon coconut oil or good-quality animal fat, plus extra for greasing
3 cloves garlic, finely chopped
1 onion, finely chopped
2 slices bacon, finely chopped
1¹⁄₃ pounds (600 g) ground beef
1 egg
½ cup (80 g) grated carrot
2 tablespoons chopped flat-leaf parsley leaves
1 teaspoon dried oregano
½ teaspoon ground cumin
1½ tablespoons tamari or coconut aminos
Pinch each of sea salt and freshly ground black pepper

TO SERVE
Tomato Ketchup (page 241)
2 tomatoes, sliced
6 gherkins, sliced
Mayonnaise (page 238) or Aïoli (page 239)
2 baby romaine lettuces, leaves separated

1. Preheat the oven to 400°F (200°C) and lightly grease a 12-hole standard muffin pan with oil or fat.

2. Heat the oil or fat in a frying pan. Add the garlic, onion, and bacon and sauté, stirring occasionally, for 6 minutes, or until browned. Remove from the heat and set aside.

3. Combine the ground beef, egg, carrot, parsley, oregano, cumin, and tamari or coconut aminos in a bowl. Add the onion mixture, season with salt and pepper, and combine well.

4. Spoon the mixture evenly into the holes of the prepared muffin tin. Bake for 15 minutes, or until the meaty muffins are perfectly juicy.

5. Spoon some tomato ketchup over each muffin, then add a slice of tomato, some gherkin, and a dollop of mayonnaise or aïoli and serve with the lettuce leaves.

AVOCADO AND SEAFOOD NORI ROLLS

It is good to see that people are looking for healthier options when it comes to lunchtime meals. Making lunch at home with minimal fuss, using the most beautiful ingredients, is better for you and better than having to pay a fortune for it. This is a favorite in our home. Swap out the fish for cooked shrimp (prawns) or smoked eel, or, if you prefer, some roast pork or beef.

Play around with different seasonal veggies, and for some added texture you can easily include broccoli rice. The kids will love these rolls in their school lunch boxes.

SERVES 4

Prep time: 30 minutes   **Cook time:** n/a
Allergens: fish, egg (mayonnaise), sesame, soy (if using)

1 avocado
2 teaspoons lemon juice
2 cups (400 g) Cauliflower Rice (see recipe below), cold
sea salt and freshly ground black pepper
6½ ounces (185 g) tuna, salmon, mackerel, or sardines in olive oil or brine, drained
4 tablespoons Mayonnaise (page 238), plus extra to serve
4 toasted nori sheets
½ Persian cucumber, deseeded and cut lengthwise into ¾-inch (1 cm) thick sticks
2 teaspoons toasted sesame seeds
Tamari or coconut aminos, to serve

1. Place the avocado and lemon juice in the bowl of a food processor and blend until smooth and creamy.

2. Transfer to a bowl, add the cauliflower rice, and mix to combine. Season with salt and pepper.

3. In another bowl, mix the fish with 2 tablespoons of the mayonnaise.

4. Place a nori sheet, rough-side up, on a counter or bamboo sushi mat. Spread one-quarter of the cauliflower rice mixture onto half the nori sheet, working from the edge closest to you and spreading it out to the sides. Layer on one-quarter of the fish mixture and cucumber and dollop on 2 teaspoons of the remaining mayonnaise. Starting with the edge closest to you, tightly wrap up the roll. If the nori roll doesn't seal, brush a little water on the inside edge of the nori sheet, then continue to roll to seal. Lightly brush the top of the nori roll with water, then sprinkle on ½ teaspoon of sesame seeds. (The light coating of water helps the sesame seeds to stick.) Repeat with the remaining nori, fillings, and sesame seeds.

5. Trim the ends of each nori roll with a sharp knife, then cut into 1-inch (2.5 cm) rounds. Serve with the tamari or coconut aminos for dipping.

Note:

- I don't recommend eating too much tuna, due to high levels of mercury. Some tuna from time to time is fine, but not every day.

CAULIFLOWER RICE

SERVES 4–6

Prep time: 8–10 minutes   **Cook time:** 3–4 minutes   **Allergens:** none

1 cauliflower, florets and stalk, coarsely
    chopped
2 tablespoons coconut oil
sea salt and freshly ground black
    pepper

1. Place the cauliflower in the bowl of a food
   processor and pulse into tiny, fine pieces that look
   like rice. Melt the coconut oil in a large frying pan
   over medium heat. Add the cauliflower and lightly
   cook for 3 or 4 minutes until softened. Season
   with salt and pepper and serve.

SALMON AND BROCCOLI NORI ROLLS

If there is one way to get broccoli into a school lunch box, here it is. The broccoli rice nori roll is the best thing since sliced paleo bread and is coming to a sushi bar near you soon! These rolls are full of nutritious goodness as we have teamed nori with avocado, wild salmon, and cucumber and added some sauerkraut on the side for good gut health. Feel free to replace the salmon with cooked shrimp or chicken or whatever animal protein you love to eat.

SERVES 4

Prep time: 20–25 minutes   **Cook time:** n/a   **Allergens:** egg, fish, sesame, soy

3½ tablespoons Mayonnaise (page 238), plus 1 tablespoon extra

2 cups (450 g) Broccoli Rice (below), cold

Sea salt and freshly ground black pepper

4 toasted nori sheets

5 ounces (150 g) sashimi-grade salmon, skin off, cut into ⅓-inch (1-cm) strips

1 Persian cucumber, deseeded and cut into ⅓-inch (1-cm) strips

1 avocado, cut into ⅓-inch (1-cm) slices

TO SERVE

Toasted sesame seeds

Chili flakes, *optional*

Tamari or coconut aminos

Sauerkraut

Wasabi

1. Place the mayonnaise and broccoli rice in a bowl and mix to combine. Season with salt and pepper.

2. Place a nori sheet, rough-side up, on a counter or bamboo sushi mat. Spread one-quarter of the broccoli rice mixture over half the nori, working from the edge closest to you and spreading it out to the sides. Arrange one-quarter of the salmon, cucumber, and avocado strips in the middle and dollop on 1 teaspoon of the extra mayonnaise. Starting with the edge closest to you, tightly wrap up the roll. If the nori roll doesn't seal, brush a little water on the inside edge of the nori sheet, then continue to roll to seal. Repeat with the remaining nori, broccoli rice, and fillings.

3. Trim the ends of each nori roll with a sharp knife and cut into 1-inch (2½ cm) rounds. Sprinkle on the toasted sesame seeds and chili flakes (if using) and serve with the tamari or coconut aminos, the sauerkraut, and the wasabi on the side.

BROCCOLI RICE

SERVES 4

Prep time: 5 minutes   **Cook time:** 5 minutes   **Allergens:** none

3 heads of broccoli (about 2 lb/900 g), coarsely chopped into florets

2 tablespoons coconut oil or good-quality animal fat

Sea salt and freshly ground black pepper

1. Place the broccoli in the bowl of a food processor and pulse into tiny, fine pieces that look like rice.

2. Heat the oil or fat in a large frying pan over medium heat, add the broccoli, and cook, stirring occasionally, for 4 or 5 minutes until tender. Season with salt and pepper and serve.

FISH AND EGG SALAD LETTUCE CUPS

School and work lunches do not have to be difficult, but they should be delicious. Here, we have taken the classic tuna and egg salad and served it in some lettuce cups. To avoid soggy lettuce, pack the salad and lettuce leaves in separate lunch boxes—you might like to pack a spoon or fork, too—and then assemble your salad cups at lunchtime.

SERVES 4

Prep time: 10 minutes   **Cook time:** 10 minutes   **Allergens:** fish, egg

6½ ounces (185 g) tuna, salmon, mackerel, or sardines in brine or olive oil, drained

6 hard-boiled eggs, chopped

3 tablespoons coarsely chopped flat-leaf parsley leaves, plus extra to serve

¼ cup (60 g) Mayonnaise (page 238), plus extra to serve

Sea salt and freshly ground black pepper

10 baby romaine lettuce leaves

1 lemon, cut into wedges

1. Place the fish, chopped egg, parsley, and mayonnaise in a bowl and gently mix to combine. Season with salt and pepper.

2. Spoon the salad into the lettuce leaf cups.

3. Top with the extra parsley, squeeze on some lemon juice, and add a dollop of extra mayonnaise.

HAM AND SALAD WRAPS

We all know that everything tastes better when it is wrapped, or perhaps it is just the ease of eating with your hands that makes a wrap more appealing. Well, whatever the reason, here we have used a simple nut-free paleo wrap to do the job and added a favorite sandwich filling.

SERVES 4

Prep time: 15 minutes   **Cook time:** 40 minutes   **Allergens:** egg

1 large beet
4 Paleo Wraps (page 227)
¼ iceberg lettuce (about 5¼ oz/150 g), leaves separated
½ cup (125 g) Mayonnaise (page 238)
1 avocado, sliced
1 carrot, grated
8 thin slices ham
1 Persian cucumber, sliced
1 large tomato, sliced
Sea salt and freshly ground black pepper

1. Place the beet in a saucepan filled with water and bring to a boil over medium heat. Reduce the heat to medium-low and cook for 40 minutes, or until cooked through. It's done when a skewer or knife inserted in the middle slips in and slides out easily.

2. Drain, allow cool to slightly, and, when cool enough to handle, peel. Allow to cool completely, then cut into ¾-inch (5-mm) thick slices and set aside.

3. Place the paleo wraps on a work surface. Divide the lettuce among the wraps, dollop on the mayonnaise, then top with the avocado, carrot, ham, cucumber, tomato, and beet. Season with salt and pepper, roll up each wrap, and serve.

BLT WITH TURKEY

I have included a few bread recipes in this book for you to try, as I know a lot of parents want to make sure that the food they pack in their kids' lunch boxes looks just like what the other kids are eating. Here is the king of all sandwiches—the BLT!

SERVES 2

Prep time: 10 minutes   **Cook time:** 5 minutes   **Allergens:** egg

1 teaspoon coconut oil or good-quality animal fat
4 slices bacon
4 sandwich-cut slices of Nut-Free Paleo Bread (page 230)
¼ cup (60 g) Aïoli (page 239) or Mayonnaise (page 238)
4 thin slices of turkey (about 2 oz/60 g)
1 tomato, sliced
2–4 baby romaine lettuce leaves, torn
1 small handful alfalfa sprouts

SMASHED AVOCADO
1 avocado
2 teaspoons lemon juice
Sea salt and freshly ground black pepper

1. Heat the oil or fat in a frying pan over medium-high heat.

2. Add the bacon and cook, turning occasionally, until golden and cooked to your liking—cook for about 5 minutes for medium-crisp.

3. To make the smashed avocado, mash the avocado with a fork or a masher until creamy but still slightly chunky. Add the lemon juice and mix until combined, then season with salt and pepper.

4. To assemble, spread half the smashed avocado on two slices of bread, then spread on half the aïoli or mayonnaise. Top with the bacon, turkey, tomato, lettuce, and alfalfa, then add the rest of the aïoli or mayonnaise and smashed avocado and finish with the remaining slices of bread.

Variation:

Use chicken instead of turkey, if you prefer.

SAUSAGE ROLL EGG WRAPS

These days we are so lucky to have butchers, delis, farmers markets, and supermarkets once again stocking and making proper sausages, one of my favorite foods to eat on a weekly basis. And sausages encased in a simple thin egg wrap is a fun way to serve them for both kids and adults. Add some raw or cooked vegetables on the side, and you have a smashing brunch, lunch, or picnic idea.

MAKES 10

Prep time: 10–15 minutes   **Cook time:** 15 minutes   **Allergens:** egg

1 tablespoon coconut oil or good-quality animal fat
10 gluten- and grain-free beef, pork, or chicken chipolatas (cocktail sausages or small sausages)
Tomato Ketchup (page 241), to serve

EGG WRAPS
6 eggs
3 tablespoons coconut milk
Sea salt and freshly ground black pepper
3½ tablespoons coconut oil or good-quality animal fat

1. To make the egg wraps, crack the eggs into a bowl, add the coconut milk and whisk with a fork until smooth. Season with a pinch of salt and pepper.

2. Heat 1 teaspoon of the oil or fat in a 8-inch (20 cm) nonstick frying pan over medium heat. Pour in about ¼ cup (60 ml) of egg mixture and tilt and swirl the pan so the mixture covers the base. Cook for 1 minute, or until the egg is just set on top. Slide onto a plate and repeat this process until all the egg mixture is used and you have 5 egg sheets.

3. Heat the oil or fat in a large frying pan over medium heat.

4. Add the sausages and cook for about 6 minutes until browned on all sides and almost cooked through. Remove the sausages from the pan and set aside.

5. Cut the egg sheets into 3 × 7-inch (8 × 18 cm) pieces and transfer to a chopping board with the short side facing you. Place a chipolata crossways at the lower edge of the egg wrap.

6. Tightly wrap, then roll the egg around the chipolata to enclose. (Trim the ends with a sharp knife, if desired).

7. Repeat with the remaining egg wraps and chipolatas.

8. Serve with the tomato ketchup.

JOY'S CHICKEN AND VEGETABLE SOUP

My mum, Joy, makes a pretty mean chicken and vegetable soup, and the girls ask for it whenever Mum has them to stay. I don't think there is a greater compliment to your cooking than getting requests for a particular dish. I asked Mum for her recipe, and she happily agreed to share it with us all. Thanks for your support and help with the girls over the last ten or so years, Mum—looking forward to many more great times together.

SERVES 6–8

Prep time: 15 minutes   **Cook time:** 3 hours   **Allergens:** none

5 chicken thighs, bone in or out
2 carrots, chopped
2 celery stalks, chopped
½ sweet potato, chopped
1 zucchini, chopped
1 onion, chopped
1 pound (450 g) pumpkin, chopped
½ teaspoon sweet paprika
½ teaspoon ground turmeric
2 quarts (8 cups/2 l) Chicken Bone
    Broth (page 33), vegetable stock, or
    water
1 handful flat-leaf parsley leaves,
    chopped
2 handfuls chopped baby spinach
    leaves
Sea salt and freshly ground black
    pepper

1. Place the chicken, carrot, celery, sweet potato, zucchini, onion, pumpkin, spices, and the broth, stock, or water in a stockpot or slow cooker, bring to a simmer, and cook on low for 3 hours.

2. Carefully remove the chicken from the soup, discard the bones and shred the meat, then set aside.

3. Using a handheld blender, blend the soup until slightly smooth (some chunks of veg are fine), then pop the chicken back in. Mix through the parsley and spinach and season with salt and pepper.

CHICKEN CAESAR SALAD

Caesar salad is one of those classic dishes adored by everyone. Adding some chicken (or turkey, pork, shrimp, or lamb) takes it from a side dish and makes it good enough to stand on its own for lunch—or dinner or even breakfast. I recommend storing the dressing separately in your lunch box and adding it when serving, so your salad doesn't go soggy. Leave off the grated macadamia to make this recipe nut free for school.

SERVES 4

Prep time: 25 minutes   **Cook time:** 16 minutes   **Allergens:** egg, nuts

4 boneless chicken thighs, skin on
2 tablespoons coconut oil or good-quality animal fat
6 slices bacon
2 heads baby romaine lettuce, leaves separated and torn
1 handful flat-leaf parsley leaves, coarsely chopped
4 soft-boiled eggs, peeled and cut in half
½ cup (70 g) Sauerkraut (see page 216)
2 macadamia nuts, finely grated, *optional*

DRESSING
½ cup (120 g) Aïoli (page 239) or Mayonnaise (page 238)
4 anchovy fillets, finely chopped
1 teaspoon lemon juice, plus extra if needed
Sea salt and freshly ground black pepper

1. To make the dressing, combine all the ingredients with 1 teaspoon of water in a small bowl. Taste and add a little more lemon juice if needed. Set aside.

2. Flatten the chicken thighs with a mallet to ensure they cook evenly. Season the skin and flesh generously with salt and pepper.

3. Melt the oil or fat in a large, heavy-based frying pan over medium-high heat. Place the chicken, skin-side down, in the pan and fry, undisturbed, for 6 to 8 minutes until crispy and golden brown. Flip the chicken over and cook for 3 minutes, or until cooked through. Remove from the pan and keep warm.

4. Add the bacon to the pan and cook over medium-high heat for 1 or 2 minutes on each side until crisp and golden. Remove from the pan and drain on paper towels. Break into bite-size pieces.

5. Arrange the lettuce and parsley in a large serving bowl. Slice the chicken, then arrange on the lettuce. Top with the bacon and eggs, add the sauerkraut, then drizzle over the dressing. Sprinkle with salt and pepper and finish with the grated macadamia (if using).

PALEO NACHOS

This is one of my girls' all-time favorite dinners, so we often send them to school the next day with leftovers. Cold Mexican ground beef is delicious with sweet potato chips or seed crackers, some guacamole, and vegetables, such as carrot, celery, tomato, and cucumber.

SERVES 4

Prep time: 25–30 minutes   **Cook time:** 22 minutes   **Allergens:** none

MEXICAN BEEF
2 tablespoons coconut oil or good-quality animal fat
1 onion, finely chopped
2 cloves garlic, finely chopped
1¼ pounds (550 g) ground beef
1 teaspoon smoked paprika
1 teaspoon chili powder
1 teaspoon ground cumin
½ teaspoon ground coriander
1½ tablespoons tomato paste
14.5 ounces (400 g) diced tomatoes
Sea salt and freshly ground black pepper

SALAD
1 baby romaine lettuce, leaves separated and torn
1 Persian cucumber, halved lengthwise and sliced
12 cherry tomatoes, halved
8 yellow teardrop tomatoes, halved
1 tablespoon apple cider vinegar
2 tablespoons extra-virgin olive oil

TO SERVE
Vegetable Crisps (we used sweet potato, page 166)
1 handful cilantro leaves
Super Guacamole (page 23)

1. To make the spicy Mexican beef, heat the oil or fat in a frying pan over medium-high heat. Add the onion and cook for 5 minutes, or until translucent. Stir in the garlic and chili and cook for 1 minute, or until fragrant. Add the beef and cook, stirring with a wooden spoon to break up any lumps, for 5 minutes until browned. Add the spices and tomato paste and cook for 1 minute, then mix in the tomatoes and ½ cup (125 ml) of water. Reduce the heat to low and simmer for 10 to 12 minutes. Season with salt and pepper.

2. To make the salad, place the lettuce, cucumber, and tomatoes in a bowl. Add the vinegar and olive oil and gently toss to coat. Season with salt and pepper.

3. Place the sweet potato crisps on serving plates or in lunch boxes, top with the spicy beef and a sprinkle of cilantro leaves, and serve with the salad and guacamole on the side.

Note:
- For added goodness, use beef or chicken broth instead of water in the Mexican beef and add some chili if desired for the grownups.

MEXICAN BEEF WITH AVOCADO TACOS

When avocados are wonderfully ripe, in season and affordable, there really is no better time to pack them in lunch boxes with assorted fillings. This Mexican beef combo and the BLT recipe (page 112) are two of my favorites to inspire you. Please feel free to create your own versions that make you and your family smile.

SERVES 2–4

Prep time: 25 minutes   **Cook time:** 22 minutes for the Mexican beef   **Allergens:** none

4 iceberg lettuce leaves, cut into cups

2 avocados, halved, seeds and skin
   removed

1 × quantity Mexican beef
   (see page 120)

½ Persian cucumber, sliced lengthwise
   and cut into matchsticks

A few cilantro sprigs

Lime wedges, to serve

TOMATO SALSA

2 tomatoes, deseeded and diced

½ red onion, finely diced

2 tablespoons chopped cilantro leaves,
   plus extra to serve

2 tablespoons lime juice

2 tablespoons extra-virgin olive oil

Sea salt and freshly ground black
   pepper

1. To make the tomato salsa, place all the ingredients in a bowl and mix well.

2. To serve, place the lettuce cups on plates or in lunch containers. Top each with an avocado half, then spoon on the spicy Mexican beef, top with the cucumber and cilantro, and serve with the tomato salsa and lime wedges on the side.

ROAST PORK WITH APPLESAUCE

A roast is one of the most enjoyable meals to cook at home. It is super easy, the kids absolutely devour it, and we get to eat the leftovers the next day. It really is a set-and-forget type of dish that takes only 10 to 15 minutes to prepare—the rest is done in the oven. Roast pork is an absolute cracker (pardon the pun); there is simply something so irresistible about eating crisp, crunchy, delicious crackling. I love to serve this with vibrant sautéed greens.

SERVES 6–8

Prep time: 25–30 minutes

Cook time: 1½ hours (plus 15 minutes resting)

Allergens: none

3 tablespoons coconut oil or other good-quality fat, melted

2 teaspoons fennel seeds

2 teaspoons sea salt

4 pounds (1.8 kg) boneless pork loin or leg

4 long, thin carrots, halved lengthwise

1 onion, unpeeled, cut into thick slices

2 cups (440 ml) chicken stock (to make your own, see 33)

1 bay leaf

APPLESAUCE

1½ tablespoons coconut oil

3 Granny Smith apples, peeled, cored and sliced

Pinch ground cinnamon

1 clove garlic, finely chopped

1. Preheat the oven to 450°F (230°C). Grease a roasting pan with 1 tablespoon of the coconut oil or other fat.

2. Using a mortar and pestle, grind the fennel seeds to a coarse powder. Mix in the salt and set aside.

3. Gently pour 1 cup (240 ml) of boiling water over the pork skin and pat dry with a paper towel. Discard the water. Diagonally and horizontally score the skin with a sharp knife in straight lines 1 inch (2½ cm) apart. Roll the pork loin up tightly and tie at regular intervals with kitchen string.

4. Put the carrots and onions in the roasting dish, then place the pork on top. Drizzle the pork skin with the oil or other fat and rub over the salt and ground fennel, covering the skin and the meat evenly.

5. Roast for 30 minutes, or until the pork skin is beginning to crackle.

6. Reduce the temperature to 350°F (180°C), then add the chicken stock and bay leaf and continue to roast for 1 hour, or until the pork is tender and just cooked through. Cover with foil and let the pork rest for 15 minutes before carving.

7. Meanwhile, to make the applesauce, melt the coconut oil in a frying pan over low heat. Add the apple and cook for 10 minutes. Stir in the cinnamon and garlic, cover and cook for 5 minutes, stirring occasionally, until the apple is soft. Puree the apple mixture in a blender or food processor. Set aside to cool.

8. Carve the pork into thick slices and serve with sautéed greens and the applesauce.

MY MEATLOAF

SERVES 6–8

Prep time: 20 minutes **Cook time:** 50 minutes (plus 10 minutes resting)
Allergens: egg, nuts

8 slices bacon

2 tablespoons coconut oil or other good-quality fat

1 large onion, diced

1 small carrot, finely diced

2 celery stalks, finely chopped

2 cloves garlic, crushed

½ zucchini, finely diced

1¾ pounds (800 g) ground grass-fed beef

4 tablespoons almond meal

4 tablespoons chopped flat-leaf parsley leaves

2 free-range organic eggs, lightly whisked

1 tablespoon Himalayan salt or sea salt

½ tablespoon freshly cracked black pepper

4 tablespoons tomato sauce (or ketchup)

1 tablespoon honey, *optional*

1 tablespoon apple cider vinegar

1. Preheat the oven to 350°F (180°C).

2. Line the base and sides of a loaf pan with a piece of parchment paper, cutting into the corners to fit and allowing the paper to extend 2 inches (5 cm) above the sides. Line the base and sides of the prepared pan with five slices of bacon, reserving the remaining slices for the top.

3. Heat a frying pan over medium heat with 2 tablespoons of coconut oil. Add the onions, carrot, and celery and cook for 5 minutes until softened, then add the garlic and zucchini and cook for a further 3 minutes. Drain out any excess liquid and allow the vegetables to cool completely in a colander.

4. Place the ground beef, almond meal, parsley, cooked vegetables, eggs, salt, and pepper in a bowl and mix until well combined.

5. Pack the meat mixture firmly into the lined loaf pan, and lay the remaining bacon slices over the top, tucking them in so they don't overhang from the sides.

6. Bake in the oven for 25 minutes.

7. Meanwhile to make the glaze, mix the tomato sauce or ketchup, honey (if using), and vinegar in a small bowl. Remove the meatloaf from the oven and baste the top of the meatloaf with the glaze. Return to the oven and continue cooking for a further 25 minutes, or until cooked through. To test if the meatloaf is cooked, insert a thermometer into the center of the meatloaf—it should reach at least 158°F (70°C).

8. Allow the meatloaf to rest in a warm place for 10 minutes before turning out of the pan—this will also allow the meat to reabsorb any cooking liquids. Slice and serve with your favorite salad or roasted vegetables.

PEPPERONI PIZZA

My daughter Indii is a huge fan of this pizza, or anything with sausage on it, for that matter. We cook this for the girls every month or so and they love coming up with their own flavor combinations.

YIELD: 1 PIZZA (SERVES 1–2)

Prep time: 10 minutes   **Cook time:** 5–10 minutes   **Allergens:** nuts, egg (pizza base)

1 Paleo pizza base (page 76)
4 tablespoons pizza sauce (page 76)
1 tablespoon chopped flat-leaf parsley leaves
6–8 cherry tomatoes, sliced
10 slices pepperoni
⅓ cup (90 g) Cashew Cheese (page 242)
Sea salt and freshly ground black pepper
2 macadamia nuts, finely grated
Mint leaves, to serve
Extra-virgin olive oil, to serve

1. Preheat the oven to 475°F (240°C). If you have a pizza stone, heat it in the oven for 15 minutes. (If you don't have a pizza stone, you can use a baking sheet, which does not require preheating.)

2. Prepare your pizza base as per the instructions on page 76. (You will cook one side of the base in the process.)

3. Spread the pizza sauce evenly over the pizza base, then sprinkle the parsley, cherry tomato slices, pepperoni, and cashew cheese over the top and season with salt and pepper. Transfer the pizza to the hot pizza stone or a baking sheet. Bake for 5 to 10 minutes until golden and crispy.

4. Sprinkle the grated macadamias over the top, garnish with the mint leaves, drizzle on a little olive oil and serve.

JOY'S BURGER

As a kid, I used to love coming home after a long surf and seeing my mum, Joy, making burger patties. Not a lot has changed since then. I still love going for long surfs and am still starving afterward. This recipe is basically the same as the one I grew up eating, but uses grilled mushrooms instead of a bread bun.

SERVES 4

Prep time: 20 minutes **Cook time:** 25 minutes **Allergens:** egg

8 large portobello mushrooms
4 tablespoons coconut oil or other good-
quality fat, melted, *divided*
Sea salt and freshly ground black pepper

PATTIES
1⅓ pounds (600 g) ground beef
½ onion, finely diced
2 cloves garlic, crushed
1 free-range egg
1 tablespoon Dijon or wholegrain mustard
Pinch dried chili flakes, *optional*
1 tablespoon chopped flat-leaf parsley
leaves
Pinch dried oregano
1 teaspoon each of Himalayan salt and
freshly ground black pepper

GARNISH
4 slices bacon, *optional*
2 onions, sliced into rings
4 free-range eggs
8 slices tomato
4 gherkins, sliced
2 carrots, grated
1 large beet, julienned
8 butter lettuce leaves
Good-quality tomato ketchup (to make
your own, see page 241), to serve
Wholegrain mustard, to serve
Aïoli (page 239), *optional*, to serve

1. Preheat the oven to 425°F (220°C). Line a baking sheet with parchment paper.

2. Destem the mushrooms and place them stem-side down on the baking sheet. Drizzle on 1 tablespoon of the coconut oil or other fat, season with salt and pepper, and bake in the oven for 10 to 15 minutes, or until the mushrooms are tender. Place the mushrooms on paper towels to remove excess moisture. Allow to cool.

3. Place all the patty ingredients in a large bowl and mix well. Shape into four patties. Heat a barbecue hotplate to medium-high. Add 2 tablespoons of the coconut oil or other fat and cook the patties, bacon (if using), and onion for 5 minutes. Stir the onion occasionally so that it doesn't burn. Turn over the patties and bacon and continue to cook for a couple of minutes until the patties are cooked through, the bacon is crisp, and the onion is caramelized. Remove from the barbecue and keep warm. Add the remaining tablespoon of coconut oil or other fat and cook the eggs to your liking. Season with salt and pepper.

4. Place the patties, mushrooms, onion, eggs, and bacon (if using) on a serving platter in the center of the table. Place the tomato, gherkins, carrot, beet, lettuce, tomato ketchup, mustard, and Aïoli (if using) in bowls and let everyone build their own burger.

COLESLAW

The older I get, the more I love and appreciate the versatility of the humble cabbage. If you think about all the delicious and healthy ways cabbage can be used, you soon realize it is pretty amazing: from gut-healing sauerkraut and spicy kimchi to cabbage rolls—so synonymous with Russian and Polish cooking—and buttery sautéed cabbage—the perfect accompaniment to roast pork. And let's not forget okonomiyaki (cabbage pancakes) from the streets of Japan and the luscious classic coleslaw found in the southern United States. Coleslaw really is one of the best salads ever created, with all the fatty goodness that comes from smothering cabbage, vegetables, and herbs in healthy aïoli.

SERVES 6

Prep time: 10 minutes   **Cook time:** n/a   **Allergens:** egg (aïoli or mayonnaise)

1 carrot, grated
¼ red onion, thinly sliced
¼ savoy cabbage, finely shredded
¼ red cabbage, finely shredded
Sea salt and freshly ground black
    pepper
1 handful dill fronds, coarsely chopped
1 handful flat-leaf parsley leaves,
    coarsely chopped
2 teaspoons finely grated lemon zest

DRESSING
Juice of 1 lemon
1 cup (240 ml) Aïoli (page 239) or
    Mayonnaise (page 238)

1. Place the carrot, onion, and shredded cabbages in a large bowl. Set aside while you make the dressing.

2. To make the dressing, combine the lemon juice and aïoli or mayonnaise in a bowl and mix well.

3. When ready to serve, season the vegetables with salt and pepper and add the herbs, lemon zest, and dressing. Toss well and serve or portion into lunch containers.

COCONUT YOGURT

This super yummy coconut yogurt is a really simple way to get good dairy-free fats and healthy probiotics into your diet. We make this once or twice a week and use it in smoothies or on top of our paleo muesli or we eat it straight out of the jar. Feel free to add in some spices, cacao, berries, or other types of in-season fruit that you love or some activated nuts and seeds. Enjoy!

MAKES 1½ QUARTS (1.5 L)

Prep time: 15 minutes, plus 12 hours fermenting time
Cook time: 5 minutes   **Allergens:** none

1 tablespoon powdered gelatin

3 tablespoons filtered water

3 (14 ½-oz/400-ml) cans coconut milk or coconut cream

1 vanilla pod, split and seeds scraped, *optional*

1–2 tablespoons honey, maple syrup, or coconut sugar

2 probiotic capsules or ¼ teaspoon nondairy starter culture, *optional*

1 tablespoon lemon juice, *optional*

Tip:

- Taste the yogurt after 12 hours. If you prefer a tangier taste, you can leave it to ferment for another couple of hours.

1. You'll need a 1½-quart (1.5-L) preserving jar with a lid for this recipe. Wash the jar and all utensils thoroughly in very hot water or run them through a hot rinse cycle in the dishwasher.

2. Place 3 tablespoons of filtered water in a small bowl, sprinkle on the gelatin, and soak for 2 minutes.

3. Place the coconut milk and vanilla seeds (if using) in a saucepan and gently heat, stirring with a spoon, over medium-low heat until just starting to simmer (194°F/90°C, if testing with a thermometer). Do not allow to boil. Immediately remove the pan from the heat. While still hot, mix in the gelatin mixture, then add the sweetener and mix well. Cover the pan with a lid and set aside to cool to lukewarm (95°F/35°C or less).

4. Pour ½ cup (120 ml) of the cooled coconut milk mixture into a sterilized bowl. Open the probiotic capsules (if using). Stir the yogurt starter or probiotic powder and lemon juice (if using) into the coconut milk in the bowl. Add the remaining coconut milk and mix well.

5. Pour the coconut milk mixture into the sterilized jar and loosely seal the lid. Ferment in a warm spot for 12 hours at 100°F–104°F (38–40°C). To maintain this temperature and allow the yogurt

to culture, wrap your jar in a dish towel, and place it on a plate in the oven with the door shut and the oven light on. The light's warmth will keep the temperature consistent. Alternatively, place the dish towel–wrapped jar in a cooler, fill a heatproof container with boiling water, and place it beside the jar—do not allow them to touch—and close the lid. Replace the boiling water halfway through the fermenting process.

6. Once fermented, the yogurt tends to form air bubbles and looks as though it has separated. Stir well and refrigerate for at least 5 hours before eating. If it separates after chilling, give it a good whisk. Store in the fridge for up to 2 weeks.

SWEET POTATO MASH

This is a hearty, luscious, satisfying accompaniment for just about any protein dish. I've used garlic and ginger for this mash, but you can add whichever spices you like to jazz it up. Try sprinkling it with fresh thyme leaves and a hint of cinnamon. One of my favorite ways to prepare and serve sweet potato mash is to add some freshly grated ginger and chopped cilantro leaves and then team it with a piece of steamed fish and Asian greens.

Remember that sweet potatoes are quite starchy, so if you are trying to lose weight or keep it off, go easy on them.

SERVES 4

Prep time: 10 minutes   **Cook time:** 25 minutes   **Allergens:** none

1 pound (450 g) sweet potato, peeled and cut into chunks
2 cloves garlic, peeled
½ cup (120 ml) coconut milk
1 tablespoon melted ghee or extra-virgin olive oil
Pinch sea salt
Freshly ground black pepper
1 teaspoon ground ginger
Chopped cilantro leaves, to serve

1. Place the sweet potato and garlic in a saucepan, cover with cold water, and bring to a boil. Reduce the heat to low, cover with a lid, and simmer for 20 minutes until tender. Drain the sweet potato and garlic, return to the pan, and mash with a fork or a wooden spoon.

2. Add the coconut milk and ghee or olive oil to the sweet potato and mix until well combined. Stir through the salt, pepper, and ginger, sprinkle over some chopped cilantro leaves, and serve immediately.

ROASTED VEGETABLES

Roasted vegetables are one of our weekly staples. We always make a huge batch of them to go with our Sunday roast, as we adore the leftovers for breakfast, lunch, dinner, or a snack. Leftover roasted veggies can quickly be turned into a soup by adding some homemade stock and some protein. You can also whisk up some eggs, pour them over your chopped leftover veggies, and bake the whole lot in the oven for a delicious frittata.

SERVES 4–6

Prep time: 10–15 minutes   **Cook time:** 30–35 minutes   **Allergens:** none

2 parsnips, halved lengthwise

1 onion, quartered

¼ pie pumpkin, cut into small wedges

7 ounces (200 g) sweet potato, cut into ¾-inch-thick (2-cm-thick) slices

2 carrots, sliced lengthwise

1 bulb garlic, halved across the cloves

4 tablespoons coconut oil or other good-quality fat, melted

Sea salt and freshly ground black pepper

8 thyme sprigs

1. Preheat the oven to 400°F (200°C).

2. Combine the parsnip, onion, pumpkin, sweet potato, carrot, and garlic in a large roasting pan and toss with the oil or fat. Season with salt and pepper.

3. Spread the vegetables over the base of the pan to form a single layer, making sure they're not bunched up. Roast for 30 to 35 minutes, or until the vegetables are tender and golden. Garnish with the thyme and serve.

ZUCCHINI CHIPS WITH HERB AÏOLI

This is a ripper of a recipe, and it's guaranteed to get your kids wolfing down zucchini like there's no tomorrow. The best way to get kids to try new foods is to get them into the kitchen to help with the preparation—they want to see and taste their handiwork. Being able to pick some zucchinis from your garden or a friend's garden would really seal the deal. The spiced seasoning adds a lovely kick to these—just go easy on it if your kids aren't into spice.

SERVES 4

Prep time: 20–25 minutes   **Cook time:** 10 minutes   **Allergens:** egg, nuts

1 egg
½ cup (120 ml) almond milk
½ cup (50 g) arrowroot
1 cup (100 g) almond meal
2 large zucchinis, cut into 3-inch
   (7.5 cm) batons, about ⅓ inch (1 cm)
   thick
1½ cups coconut oil, tallow, or duck fat

HERB AÏOLI
1 tablespoon finely chopped flat-leaf
   parsley leaves
½ teaspoon finely grated lemon zest
1 cup (250 g) Aïoli (page 239)

SPICED SEASONING
3 tablespoons sea salt 2 tablespoons
   paprika
1 tablespoon garlic powder
1 teaspoon ground cumin
1 teaspoon ground white pepper
½ teaspoon chili powder
½ teaspoon celery salt

1. To make the spiced seasoning, combine all the ingredients in a small bowl and stir well. Set aside until ready to use.

2. To make the herb aïoli, place the ingredients in a bowl and mix well. Refrigerate until required.

3. Whisk the egg in a bowl with the almond milk until well combined. Place the arrowroot and almond meal into two small, shallow bowls.

4. Individually coat each zucchini stick in the arrowroot, shaking off any excess. Dip the coated zucchini in the egg mixture then roll in the almond meal, ensuring it is coated evenly. If you miss some patches, simply dab a little more egg mixture onto the dry areas and coat again with the almond meal.

5. Heat the coconut oil in a large, deep frying pan over medium heat. Test if the oil is hot enough by dropping in a small piece of zucchini—if the oil begins to bubble around the zucchini, it has reached the ideal temperature. Add the zucchini chips in batches, and cook for 2 minutes on each side, or until golden brown and crisp.

6. Remove the chips from the pan using metal tongs or a slotted spoon, and transfer to paper towels to drain. Allow the chips to cool slightly before serving.

7. Sprinkle with a little spiced seasoning and serve with herb aïoli. The leftover spiced seasoning can be stored in an airtight container in the pantry for several months.

ROASTED TURKEY WITH HERB MARINADE

I am pleased to learn that some well-intentioned farmers in Australia (and in the United States) are now producing free-range, hormone- and antibiotic-free turkeys—it is a step in the right direction. I have created a basic but delicious recipe for roasted turkey here—please feel free to play around with stuffing ingredients and accompaniments to further enhance it. You will need to start this recipe a day ahead. And if your turkey is frozen, thaw in the fridge for approximately 3 days. Once thawed, leave in the fridge until ready to cook.

SERVES 8

Prep time: 30–40 minutes, plus 24 hours to marinate **Cook time:** 3¼ hours
Allergens: nuts, sesame

8-pound (3.6-kg) turkey
Good-quality fat, melted
2 carrots, sliced lengthwise
1 onion, sliced
4 cloves garlic, peeled
5 fresh bay leaves
5 cups (1.2 l) chicken stock (to make your own, see page 33)
2 tablespoons tapioca flour, mixed with 3 tablespoons water

MARINADE
2 large handfuls mint leaves
2 large handfuls curly parsley leaves
2 large handfuls cilantro leaves
4 cloves garlic, peeled
1 cup (240 ml) lemon juice
1 cup (240 ml) white wine
7 ounces (200 g) good-quality fat, melted
2 teaspoons ground cumin
Salt and freshly ground black pepper

1. To make the marinade, combine all the ingredients in a food processor and blend until smooth. Put the turkey in a large shallow dish, pat dry with a paper towel, and pour the marinade over it. Massage the marinade all over the turkey and inside the cavity, cover with plastic wrap, and place in the fridge for 24 hours. Every few hours, massage the marinade onto the bird.

2. The next day, remove the turkey from the fridge and allow to come to room temperature (this will take about 1 hour). Preheat the oven to 450°F (230°C).

3. To make the stuffing, heat the fat in a saucepan over medium heat. Add the onion and cook until soft, about 5 minutes. Crush the garlic confit and add to the pan, along with the bacon. Cook until just starting to color, about 3 to 5 minutes. Remove from the heat and set aside to cool. Add the remaining ingredients and mix until combined.

4. Fill the turkey cavity with the stuffing, cross the legs over, and tie with kitchen string. Place in a large roasting pan and pour in the marinade. Rub with some melted fat and season with salt and pepper. Add the carrot, onion, garlic, and bay leaves, cover with foil, and place in the oven. Reduce the temperature to 350°F (180°C) and

STUFFING

2 tablespoons good-quality fat, melted

1 onion, finely chopped

**4 garlic confit cloves (to make your
own, see page 244)**

3 slices bacon, diced

4 tablespoons chopped curly parsley

3 tablespoons dukkah

1 pound (450 g) ground pork

1 teaspoon finely grated lemon zest

roast, pouring the pan juices over the turkey a few times, for about 2 hours. To brown the skin, remove the foil in the final 40 minutes. The turkey is cooked once the juices run clear when the inside of the thigh is pierced with a skewer. Cooking time may vary—it should take about 13 minutes per pound (40 minutes per kilogram). Transfer the turkey to a large serving platter, cover with foil, and rest for 20 minutes.

5. To make the gravy, place the chicken stock in a saucepan over medium heat and simmer until reduced by half, about 20 minutes. Skim the fat from the surface of the juices in the roasting pan with the vegetables and discard. Pour the tapioca mixture and stock into the roasting pan and mix well. Bring to a boil over medium heat, stirring occasionally. Reduce the heat to low and simmer until the sauce thickens.

6. Strain into a gravy jug or bowl. Carve the turkey and serve with the gravy.

JUMBO SHRIMP
WITH PRESERVED LEMON GUACAMOLE

Shrimp and avocado are a divine combination, and it is incredibly easy to create delicious variations of this simple recipe. Start by sourcing the freshest, plumpest prawns you can get your hands on, find some gorgeous ripe avocados, and then all you need to do is add your favorite dressing, marinade, sauce, or mayonnaise. Finish with some herbs and maybe some nuts and seeds and you have a pretty fabulous dish. In this version, I've added preserved lemon for a unique twist on guacamole that will have your guests or family thinking you spent hours in the kitchen.

SERVES 4

Prep time: 20 minutes   **Cook time:** 15–17 minutes   **Allergens:** shellfish

16 raw jumbo shrimp (king prawns)
3 tablespoons lemon-infused extra-
    virgin olive oil, plus extra to serve
1 tablespoon lemon juice
1 teaspoon chopped dill
Sea salt and freshly ground black
    pepper
1 red bell pepper, diced
1 handful cilantro leaves
1 handful dill leaves

GUACAMOLE
½ red bell pepper
2 avocados, sliced
1 Roma tomato, deseeded and diced
1 small red chili, deseeded and finely
    chopped, *optional*
¼ red onion, finely chopped
1 tablespoon finely chopped preserved
    lemon
1 tablespoon chopped cilantro leaves
2 tablespoons lemon juice
2 tablespoons lemon-infused extra-
    virgin olive oil

1. Cook the shrimp in salted boiling water for 2 or 3 minutes, or until pink and firm. Transfer to a bowl of iced water to cool completely. Peel and devein, keeping the tails intact.

2. Combine the olive oil, lemon juice, and dill in a bowl and season with salt and pepper. Whisk to combine, then add the shrimp and toss until well coated. Cover with plastic wrap and marinate for 5 minutes in the fridge.

3. Preheat the oven to 400°F (200°C).

4. To make the guacamole, place the bell pepper, skin-side up, on a baking sheet. Roast in the oven for 10 to 15 minutes, or until the skin blisters and blackens. Place the bell pepper in a bowl, cover with plastic wrap, and set aside to steam for 5 minutes.

5. Peel and discard the skin, then chop the flesh. Combine the avocado, roasted bell pepper, tomato, chili (if using), onion, preserved lemon, cilantro, lemon juice, and olive oil in a bowl and gently mix. Season with salt and pepper to taste.

6. Spoon the guacamole onto a serving platter, top with the marinated shrimp, garnish with the bell pepper, cilantro, and dill and serve with a drizzle of extra oil.

BEEF BONE BROTH

MAKES 4¼ QUARTS (4 L)

Prep time: 15 minutes (plus 1 hour standing time) **Cook time:** 6–12 hours
Allergens: none

About 4¹/₃ pounds (2 kg) beef knuckle and marrow bones
1 calf foot, chopped into pieces, *optional*
3 tablespoons apple cider vinegar
3¹/₃ pounds (1.5 kg) meaty beef rib or neck bones
3 onions, coarsely chopped
3 carrots, coarsely chopped
3 celery stalks, coarsely chopped
2 leeks, white part only, coarsely chopped
3 thyme sprigs
2 bay leaves
1 teaspoon black peppercorns, crushed
1 bulb garlic, cut in half horizontally
2 large handfuls flat-leaf parsley stalks

1. Place the knuckle and marrow bones and calf foot (if using) in a stockpot, add the vinegar, and pour in 5¼ quarts (5 l) of cold water, or enough to cover. Set aside for 1 hour to help draw out the nutrients from the bones. Remove the bones from the water, reserving the water.

2. Preheat the oven to 350°F (180°C).

3. Place the knuckle and marrow bones, calf foot (if using), and meaty bones in a few large roasting pans and roast in the oven for 30 to 40 minutes until well browned. Return all the bones to the pot and add the vegetables.

4. Pour the fat from the roasting pans into a saucepan, add 1 quart (1 l) of the reserved water, place over high heat, and bring to a simmer, stirring with a wooden spoon to loosen any coagulated juices. Add this liquid to the bones and vegetables. If necessary, add the remaining reserved water to the pot to just cover the bones—the liquid should come no higher than ¾ inch (2 cm) below the rim of the pot, as the volume will increase slightly during cooking.

5. Bring the broth to a boil, skimming off the scum that rises to the top.

6. Reduce the heat to low and add the thyme, bay leaves, peppercorns, and garlic. Simmer for 12 to 24 hours. Just before finishing, add the parsley and simmer for 10 minutes. Strain the broth into a large container, cover, and place in the fridge overnight. Remove the congealed fat that rises to the top and reserve for cooking; it will keep in the fridge for up to 1 week or in the freezer for up to 3 months.

7. Transfer the thick and gelatinous broth to smaller airtight containers and place in the fridge or, for long-term storage, the freezer. The broth can be stored in the fridge for 3 or 4 days or frozen for up to 3 months.

FISH BONE BROTH

Whenever you have a whole fish, make sure you keep the head and bones so that you can make a delicious broth. Fish bone broth can be used as an aromatic base to create the most amazing soups and curries. All you need to do is add seafood, vegetables, spices, and herbs and, voilà, you have dinner in mere minutes.

MAKES ABOUT 3⅛ QUARTS (3 L)

Prep time: 10 minutes   **Cook time:** 3–4 hours   **Allergens:** fish

3 or 4 non-oily fish carcasses and heads (such as snapper, barramundi, or kingfish)
2 celery stalks, coarsely chopped
2 onions, coarsely chopped
1 carrot, coarsely chopped
2 tablespoons apple cider vinegar
1 handful thyme and flat-leaf parsley sprigs
3 fresh or dried bay leaves

1. Place the fish carcasses and heads in a stockpot or very large saucepan, add the veggies and apple cider vinegar, and cover with 3⅔ quarts (3.5 l) of cold water.

2. Bring to a boil, skimming off the scum and any impurities as they rise to the top. Tie the herbs together with kitchen string and add to the broth.

3. Reduce the heat to low, cover and simmer for 3–4 hours.

4. Remove the fish carcasses and heads with tongs or a slotted spoon. Strain the broth into storage containers, cover, and chill in the refrigerator. Remove the congealed fat that rises to the top. (Store it in a glass container in the fridge for up to 2 weeks and use it for frying and sautéing.) The broth can be stored in the refrigerator for up to 4 days or frozen for up to 3 months.

HEMP SEED PORRIDGE WITH BLUEBERRY COMPOTE

Hemp seeds are the perfect keto choice for porridge, as they are roughly 70 percent fat, 25 percent protein, and 5 percent carbs. When teamed with your choice of milk—such as coconut, nut, or hemp—and the addition of low-carb fruits like berries, you create a keto breakfast that is a fun way to get healthy plant-based fats into your diet. Always try to source wild, organic blueberries if possible.

SERVES 2

Prep time: 10 minutes   **Cook time:** 12 minutes   **Allergens:** nuts (if using nut milk)

1 cup plus 1 tablespoon (150 g) hemp seeds

2 cups (480 ml) coconut or plant-based milk of your choice, plus extra to serve

2 tablespoons shredded coconut

2 tablespoons ground flaxseeds

1 tablespoon chia seeds

1 teaspoon manuka honey or sweetener of your choice (liquid stevia, xylitol, monk fruit sweetener), to taste

Pinch sea salt

½ teaspoon vanilla powder or paste

BLUEBERRY COMPOTE

1⅓ cups (200 g) blueberries (fresh or frozen)

1 tablespoon manuka honey or sweetener of your choice (liquid stevia, xylitol, monk fruit sweetener), to taste.

1. To make the blueberry compote, place half the blueberries and the honey or sweetener in a small saucepan over low heat. Cook for 5 minutes until the blueberries have slightly broken down. Remove from the heat, stir through the remaining berries, and allow to cool.

2. Combine the hemp seeds, milk of your choice, coconut, flaxseeds, chia seeds, honey or sweetener, and salt in a small saucepan over medium-low heat. Cook, stirring frequently, for 5 to 7 minutes, or until thickened. Stir in the vanilla.

3. Transfer the porridge to serving bowls, pour over some extra milk, then spoon over the blueberry compote and serve.

NIC'S AVOCADO TOAST WITH POACHED EGGS

SERVES 4

Prep time: 5 minutes   **Cook time:** 5 minutes   **Allergens:** egg

2 avocados, diced
⅓ cup (80 ml) white or apple cider
  vinegar
8 eggs
8 slices Nut-Free Paleo Bread
  (page 230), toasted
Sea salt and freshly ground black
  pepper

DRESSING

1 tablespoon chopped cilantro leaves
2 tablespoons lime juice
3 tablespoons extra-virgin olive oil
Sea salt and freshly ground black
  pepper

1. To make the dressing, place the cilantro, lime juice, and olive oil in a bowl and mix to combine. Season with salt and pepper. Set aside until needed.

2. Place the avocado and 2 tablespoons of the dressing in a bowl, crush lightly with a fork, then mix to combine. Season with salt and pepper.

3. Meanwhile, pour the vinegar into a saucepan of boiling salted water, then reduce the heat to medium-low so the water is just simmering. Crack an egg into a cup. Using a wooden spoon, stir the simmering water in one direction to form a whirlpool and drop the egg into the center. Repeat with the remaining eggs and cook for 3 minutes for runny yolks, or cook to your liking. Remove the eggs with a slotted spoon and place on a paper towel to drain.

4. To serve, spread the avocado over the toast, then top with a poached egg. Drizzle over the remaining dressing and finish with a sprinkle of salt and pepper.

AVOCADO SMASH ON TOAST WITH SMOKED SALMON

It may seem a little clichéd to include avocado toast here, but I am a sucker for it and love to make it for the whole family. What we put with ours changes all the time; sometimes it's crispy bacon, at other times poached eggs or cooked prawns, and one of our favorites is smoked salmon and roe with sprouts, watercress, or herbs. It's always good to give your avocado a generous hit of lemon juice to cut through the richness. If you don't have time to make keto bread, feel free to roast mushrooms instead or cook eggs just the way you like them to go with the avocado smash.

SERVES 4

Prep time: 10 minutes   **Cook time:** n/a   **Allergens:** fish

8 slices Nut-Free Paleo Bread
  (page 230), toasted
12 slices smoked salmon
2 tablespoons salted baby capers,
  rinsed and patted dry
1 small handful alfalfa sprouts
1 small handful baby kale sprouts or
  sprouts of your choice
3 tablespoons salmon roe
Extra-virgin olive oil, for drizzling
½ red onion, very finely sliced, *optional*
1 lemon, cut into wedges

AVOCADO SMASH
2 avocados, coarsely chopped
1 teaspoon lemon juice, or to taste
1 tablespoon extra-virgin olive oil
Sea salt and freshly ground black
  pepper

1. Place all the avocado smash ingredients in a bowl and mash with a fork. Taste and season with a little more salt and pepper if needed.

2. Spread the avocado smash over the toast, then top with the smoked salmon. Sprinkle on the capers, alfalfa, and kale sprouts, then spoon over the salmon roe. Drizzle over some olive oil and finish with a sprinkle of salt and pepper. Serve with the red onion (if using) and lemon wedges on the side.

SLOW-COOKED SOUTHERN BRISKET

On my first visit to the southern United States about ten years ago, I was truly blown away by the standard of cooking, the quality of produce, and the local chefs' depth of knowledge. One of the meals I got to experience was a proper American slow-cooked brisket barbecue. And, I have to say, it was up there with the best meat I have ever had the pleasure of eating. Serve this with your roasted vegetables, salad, or slaw.

SERVES 8

Prep time: 10 minutes   **Cook time:** 12½ hours   **Allergens:** none

2 tablespoons melted coconut oil or good-quality animal fat
1 (6½-lb/3-kg) piece beef brisket
Sea salt and freshly ground black pepper
4 shallots, unpeeled, halved lengthwise
1 bulb garlic, halved horizontally and broken into 8 pieces
8 thyme sprigs
1½ cups (350 ml) Beef or Chicken Bone Broth (page 146 or 33)

BARBECUE SPICE RUB
1 tablespoon sea salt
2 tablespoons smoked paprika
2 teaspoons freshly ground black pepper
1 tablespoon onion powder
1 tablespoon garlic powder

1. Preheat the oven to 210°F (100°C).

2. Combine the barbecue spice rub ingredients in a small bowl.

3. Rub the coconut oil or fat over the brisket, then lightly season with salt and pepper.

4. Heat a large roasting pan over high heat, add the brisket, and sear on all sides for 3 or 4 minutes until browned. Place the brisket, fat-side up, on a large plate. When cool enough to handle, evenly coat the seared brisket with 3 tablespoons of the barbecue spice rub.

5. Arrange the shallot, garlic, and thyme in the pan in a single layer, place the brisket on top, and pour in the broth. Cover the brisket firmly with a damp piece of parchment paper, then tightly cover the pan with a double layer of foil. Roast for 12 hours, or until the brisket is tender. Place the brisket on a plate, cover loosely, and rest for 15 to 30 minutes, keeping warm.

6. Thickly carve the brisket and serve.

Note:
- You can store the remaining barbecue spice rub in an airtight container in the pantry for up to 6 months.

CRACKLING CHICKEN

Michelle Tam, author of the food blog and cookbook *Nom Nom Paleo*, is loved by millions around the world for her no-nonsense approach to cooking paleo food. Mich prepared this recipe for me at her home in San Francisco while I was filming the first series of *The Paleo Way* for TV. I love the simplicity of this cooking technique, and I also love to cook duck breast this way so it gets really crispy skin. Serve with a generous salad or cooked green vegetables and some fermented vegetables for good measure.

SERVES 4

Prep time: 25 minutes   **Cook time:** 20 minutes   **Allergens:** none

8 chicken thigh fillets, skin left on
1 tablespoon sea salt
2 teaspoons coconut oil or other good-quality fat
2 teaspoons spice mix of your choice (I like using a Cajun or Moroccan mix), *optional*
Lemon wedges, to serve

1. Flatten the chicken thighs with a mallet to ensure they cook evenly. Season the skin with salt.

2. Melt the oil or fat in a large, heavy-based frying pan over medium-high heat. Place four of the chicken thighs, skin-side down, in the hot pan and season the exposed side with 1 teaspoon of the seasoning (if using). If your seasoning doesn't include salt, you may wish to add a little.

3. Fry the chicken, undisturbed, for 6 to 8 minutes until crispy and golden brown. Flip the chicken over and cook for 3 minutes, or until cooked through. Remove from the pan and keep warm. Repeat with the remaining chicken.

4. Serve with the lemon wedges and your favorite vegetables or salad.

Tip:

- If you are using duck, make sure you cook it over very low heat to allow the fat to render and give you the most amazingly crispy skin.

SIRLOIN STEAK WITH LEMON, SALT, AND OLIVE OIL

The one piece of advice I give parents who ask me about what to feed their children is always the same: Feed them more meat and seafood! The reason for this is that children are growing, and the thing that they need for their development is good-quality protein and fat from healthy animals as their number one food source. My own children have thrived from eating this way and they are now very healthy and strong eighteen- and nineteen-year-olds. A simple cooked steak has been one of their bedrock meals and the one they still love to eat with me.

SERVES 2

Prep time: 5 minutes   **Cook time:** 30 minutes   **Allergens:** none

1 bulb garlic, halved horizontally
2 (7-oz/200 g) sirloin steaks
1 tablespoon coconut oil or good-quality animal fat, melted
Sea salt and freshly ground black pepper
1 lemon, halved

1. Preheat the oven to 350°F (180°C).

2. Place the garlic on a baking sheet and roast for 25 to 30 minutes, or until golden and tender. Heat a barbecue grill plate to hot or a large chargrill pan over high heat.

3. Brush the steaks with the coconut oil or animal fat and season with salt and pepper. Cook the steaks on one side for 3 minutes, or until golden, then flip and cook on the other side for 3 minutes for medium-rare (or cook to your liking). Place the steaks on a plate, loosely cover, and rest for 4 to 6 minutes, keeping warm.

4. Meanwhile, cook the lemon halves, cut-side down, for 6 minutes, or until charred. Carve the steak into thick slices and serve with the charred lemon and roasted garlic.

SIMPLE OVEN-BAKED SALMON

Cooking does not need to be difficult. In fact, my favorite dishes are usually the simplest. A beautiful piece of seafood or meat, simply cooked, like this oven-baked salmon, brings so much joy to myself and my family, and it is stress free. If your child isn't a huge fan of salmon (yet), then simply cook a different type of fish or meat that they love and serve it with a wedge of lemon and/or some good-quality mayonnaise and enjoy their smiles as you all eat.

SERVES 4

Prep time: 2 minutes   **Cook time:** 8 minutes   **Allergens:** fish

4 (5¼-oz/150-g) salmon fillets, skin on, pin-boned
2 tablespoons melted coconut oil or good-quality animal fat
Sea salt and freshly ground black pepper
Lemon wedges, to serve

1. Preheat the oven to 400°F (200°C).

2. Heat a heavy-based ovenproof frying pan over high heat until very hot. Brush the fish with the coconut oil or fat, season with salt and pepper, and cook, skin-side down, for 30 to 60 seconds or until crispy.

3. Transfer the pan to the oven and cook the salmon, still with the skin side down, for 3½ to 4 minutes for medium-rare (or until cooked to your liking) and until the skin is golden and crisp.

4. Flip the salmon, skin-side up, onto a plate and allow to rest for 2 or 3 minutes, keeping warm. At this point the salmon will be perfectly cooked, slightly pink and moist in the middle. Serve with some lemon wedges.

SHRIMP, GINGER, AND BROCCOLI STIR-FRY

Who doesn't love a good stir-fry? They're super quick to put together and taste amazing and you can take them in so many different directions. Whip up this simple and delicious shrimp stir-fry in less than ten minutes. Serve with cauliflower rice if desired.

SERVES 4

Prep time: 25 minutes   **Cook time:** 10 minutes   **Allergens:** shellfish, fish, soy

3 tablespoons coconut oil or good-quality animal fat, *divided*

1¼ pounds (550 g) raw medium shrimp (prawns), shelled and deveined, tails left intact

2-inch (5-cm) piece ginger, cut into matchsticks

1 tablespoon finely chopped lemongrass, pale part only

½ onion, sliced

8 scallions, white parts only, cut into 2-inch (5-cm) lengths (reserve the green part for other recipes)

1 head of broccoli (about 10½ oz/300 g), broken into florets

4 cloves garlic, thinly sliced

1 long red chili, thinly sliced, *optional*

2 tablespoons tamari

2 tablespoons fish sauce

2 teaspoons coconut sugar, honey or monk fruit sweetener, *optional*

1 cup (240 ml) Chicken Bone Broth (page 33)

1½ tablespoons tapioca flour, mixed with 1 tablespoon water

2 handfuls water spinach or baby spinach leaves

1 handful Thai basil leaves

1. Heat 1 tablespoon of the coconut oil or fat in a wok or large frying pan over medium-high heat. Add the shrimp, in batches, and cook for 30 seconds on each side. Remove from the pan and set aside until needed.

2. Wipe the wok or pan clean, add the remaining coconut oil or fat, and place over medium-high heat. Add the ginger, lemongrass, onion, scallions, broccoli, garlic, and chili and stir-fry for 3 or 4 minutes until fragrant and starting to color slightly.

3. Mix in the tamari, fish sauce, sweetener (if using), broth, and tapioca mixture and simmer for 1 minute, or until the sauce thickens. Add the shrimp and mix through until they are just cooked. Remove from the heat, toss through the spinach and Thai basil leaves, and serve.

VEGETABLE CRISPS

These vegetable crisps are a whole lot of fun. You could simply make them with one type of vegetable, which would be perfectly delicious or, if you want to go the whole hog, you could do a variety, as we have done here. I guarantee they won't last long though, so make sure you make enough to go around.

SERVES 4–6

Prep time: 10 minutes   **Cook time:** 50 minutes   **Allergens:** none

2 cups (500 ml) coconut oil or good-quality animal fat
1 sweet potato (about 8½ oz/240 g), thinly sliced with a mandolin or sharp knife
1 large parsnip (about 10 oz/280 g), thinly sliced with a mandolin or sharp knife
Sea salt
½ × quantity Kale Chips (page 167)

BEET CHIPS
2 beets
2 tablespoons coconut oil, melted
Sea salt

1. Preheat the oven to 275°F (130°C). Line three or four large baking sheets with parchment paper.

2. To make the beet chips, peel the beets (wearing gloves to avoid staining your hands), and, using a mandolin, cut into ⅛-inch-thick (2-mm-thick) slices. If you don't have a mandolin, simply slice thinly with a sharp knife. Place the beet slices in a large bowl and, still wearing gloves, gently toss

with the oil and season with salt. Arrange a single layer of beet slices on the baking sheets and bake for 30 minutes. Rotate the baking sheets and cook for a further 20 minutes until the beet slices are crisp at the edges, keeping a close eye on them to prevent burning. (The beet chips may need a few minutes longer, but they will crisp up as they cool.) Remove from the oven. Store in an airtight container in the pantry for up to 2 weeks.

3. Melt the oil or fat in a large saucepan over medium-high heat until the temperature reaches about 325°F (160°C). (To test, drop a sweet potato or parsnip slice into the hot oil; if it starts bubbling straight away, it is ready.) Fry the sliced sweet potato and parsnip separately in batches for 2 to 3½ minutes until just starting to color. Remove from the oil, drain on paper towels, and season with salt. Repeat with the remaining sliced vegetables.

4. Keep a close eye when cooking at all times, as the crisps can burn very quickly. Store in an airtight container in the pantry for up to 3 days.

5. To serve, gently mix the kale and beet chips with the crisp sweet potato and parsnip.

• • • • • • • • • • • • • • • • • •

KALE CHIPS

SERVES 2–4

Prep time: 5 minutes   **Cook time:** 40 minutes   **Allergens:** none

1 bunch of kale (about 10½ oz/300 g)
1 tablespoon coconut oil, melted
½ teaspoon of your favorite spice
  (such as curry powder, ras el hanout,
  smoked paprika, ground cumin, or
  ground turmeric), *optional*
Sea salt

1. Preheat the oven to 250°F (120°C). Line a baking sheet with parchment paper.

2. Wash the kale thoroughly in cold water and pat dry. Remove and discard the tough central stems, then cut the leaves into smaller pieces.

3. In a large bowl, toss the kale with some coconut oil, spices (if using), and salt—go easy on the salt as a little goes a long way. Spread the kale on the baking sheet in a single layer; do not overcrowd. Use more than one baking sheet, if required. Roast the kale for 35 to 40 minutes until crispy. Serve immediately or store in an airtight container in the pantry for up to 2 weeks.

SHEPHERD'S PIE

One of my favorite childhood foods was the good old meat pie with tomato sauce. Little did I know then how poorly produced they were, using pastry made from white flour and margarine. Hopefully the meat back then was grass-fed, but the fillers to make it bind would have been terrible thickening agents. This recipe has none of the nasties of commercially produced pies, but lots of added goodies in the form of liver and marrow.

SERVES 6

Prep time: 12 minutes   **Cook time:** 45 minutes   **Allergens:** nuts

1 large cauliflower (about 2¼ lb/1 kg), chopped
4 tablespoons cold-pressed, virgin coconut oil or other good-quality fat
¾ teaspoon ground cumin
1 onion, diced
4 cloves garlic, diced
2 celery sticks, diced
2 carrots, diced
1⅓ pounds (600 g) grass-fed ground beef
3 free-range chicken livers (sinew removed), finely chopped
2½ tablespoons tomato paste
1 teaspoon chopped thyme leaves
1½ cups (350 ml) beef broth (page 146)
Freshly ground black pepper
2 macadamia nuts (activated if possible, see page 245)
3 tablespoons chopped parsley, plus extra to serve

1. Preheat the oven to 350°F (180°C).

2. Fill a large saucepan with water and bring to a boil. Add the cauliflower and boil until tender (about 10 minutes). Transfer the cooked cauliflower to a colander and drain.

3. Heat 2 tablespoons of the oil in a large frying pan or saucepan over medium heat. Add the cumin, onion, garlic, celery, and carrot and cook for 5 minutes or until the vegetables soften and begin to brown. Add the ground beef and liver, and cook until the meat has browned. Add the tomato paste and thyme and cook for 1 minute. Pour in the broth and simmer for 10 minutes, stirring occasionally. Season with freshly ground black pepper. Meanwhile, place the cooked cauliflower in a food processor with the remaining 2 tablespoons of oil and blend until smooth. Season to taste with pepper.

4. To assemble, spread the meat mixture over the base of one large ovenproof dish or six small ones. Top with an even layer of cauliflower puree. Bake for 30 minutes, or until lightly golden.

5. To serve, finely grate the macadamias over the top and sprinkle with parsley.

NIC'S CHOPPED SALAD

My wife, Nic, is the salad queen in our house and is always inventing new ways to spice them up. She'll take a simple salad like this and add some slowly toasted, spiced nuts and seeds to create another textural element. So feel free to use this salad as the starting point and add your own combination of nuts and seeds or even protein like smoked wild fish, leftover roast chicken, or pork.

SERVES 4–6

Prep time: 25 minutes   **Cook time:** n/a   **Allergens:** none

3 tomatoes, deseeded and diced

1 red bell pepper, diced

2 Persian cucumbers, diced

2 scallions, thinly sliced

1 baby romaine lettuce, chopped

1 cup (75 g) red cabbage, shredded

2 tablespoons chopped flat-leaf parsley
  leaves

2 tablespoons chopped cilantro leaves

1 tablespoon chopped mint leaves

1 avocado, diced

¼ cup (40 g) pumpkin seeds

⅓ cup (40 g) sunflower seeds

DRESSING

1 teaspoon wholegrain mustard or
  Dijon mustard

2 tablespoons sherry vinegar

1 tablespoon lemon juice

4 tablespoons extra-virgin olive oil

Salt and freshly ground black pepper

1. To make the dressing, place the mustard, vinegar, and lemon juice in a bowl and whisk to combine. Slowly add the oil in a thin, steady stream and whisk until incorporated. Season with salt and pepper.

2. Place all the salad ingredients in a bowl, add the dressing, and gently toss. Season with salt and pepper. Allow the salad to stand for 10 minutes before serving.

PART 3
DESSERTS

Desserts are what I like to embrace as a delicious treat and another beautiful way to celebrate with my family and loved ones.

It is always good to remember that children can develop eating habits very easily, and one of the main things I have learned over the years is that too much "sweet" food in a child's diet can create that habit of wanting more sweet foods and less of the savory.

So a lot of common sense and observing your children's eating behavior will no doubt help you and them on the journey. The recipes in this dessert section are wonderful grain- and dairy-free options for birthday parties, celebrations, hot summer days, or whenever you want to include them. Some of the recipes are low carbohydrate and won't spike blood sugar levels and others are more at the opposite end of spectrum and have a higher carbohydrate amount, so play around with them and see how your child reacts to them after they have enjoyed them to see if their behavior changes.

COCONUT AND GELATIN POTS WITH BLUEBERRY

I am not a huge fan of sweets, because once that sugar-craving monster steps into our lives, it's very hard for us to kick it out. That being said, I think this simple treat is a healthy option if you want to make something special for a birthday party celebration. Note that coconut cream works better than coconut milk for this recipe due to its higher fat content.

SERVES 5

Prep time: 10 minutes (plus 4 hours setting)   **Cook time:** 3 minutes   **Allergens:** none

1½ teaspoons grass-fed gelatin powder

2 cups (500 ml) coconut cream or coconut milk

¼ teaspoon vanilla bean powder

⅛ teaspoon green leaf stevia powder

1 cup (150 g) blueberries (fresh or frozen), plus extra to serve

1. Sprinkle the gelatin over the coconut cream or milk at room temperature and leave to sit for 2 minutes to absorb the liquid and expand.

2. Place the coconut cream mixture in a saucepan over medium heat. Add the vanilla and bring to a simmer, stirring constantly. Immediately remove from the heat, then mix in the stevia. Allow to cool completely before pouring into the molds.

3. Divide the blueberries evenly between five 4-ounce (120-ml) ramekins or molds. Pour in the cooled coconut cream mixture until it almost reaches the rim. Transfer the ramekins to the refrigerator and leave for 4 hours, or until set. Sprinkle some more blueberries on top and serve.

Note:

- Great Lakes makes a really good grass-fed gelatin.

BANANA BERRY ICE CREAM

Ice cream is the ultimate comfort food, and this delicious, healthy version can be made so quickly and easily. You can use any frozen organic fruit.

SERVES 2–4
YIELD: ABOUT 1¼ POUNDS (550G)

Prep time: 5 minutes   **Cook time:** n/a   **Allergens:** none

2 frozen bananas
1⅓ cup (160 g) frozen organic mixed berries
4 tablespoons coconut cream
Pinch ground cinnamon

SOME OTHER GREAT FRUIT COMBOS
Passionfruit and mango
Papaya and berries
Banana and mango

1. Place all the ingredients in a blender and pulse until you have an ice cream–like consistency. That's it!

Tips:

- Sprinkle some chia seeds or dried coconut on top for texture.

- It's always a good idea to have a couple of ripe bananas in your freezer. Just peel and slice them first, and pop them in a freezer container.

CHIA SEED PUDDINGS WITH FRESH BERRIES

Berries are our favorite fruit due to their low fructose content, so we love to indulge in them when they're in season. They're divine in this chia and young coconut mix. If they are out of season, thawed frozen berries will do just fine.

SERVES 2–4

Prep time: 5 minutes (plus 2 hours setting)   **Cook time:** n/a   **Allergens:** none

1 young coconut
½ cup (125 ml) organic coconut cream
    or coconut milk
¼ cup (50 g) chia seeds
Pinch green leaf stevia powder
½ cup (80 g) raspberries, blueberries,
    and chopped fresh strawberries

Note:

• If your child has a sensitive tummy, be mindful that this recipe contains a lot of chia seeds.

1. Cut a square opening in the top of the coconut using a large, sharp knife or cleaver. Pour the coconut water into a measuring cup. Scrape and scoop the coconut meat out of the shell with a spoon and coarsely chop the meat into smaller pieces.

2. Place the coconut meat in a food processor with ½ cup (125 ml) of coconut water, and process to a smooth, thick puree.

3. Pour the puree into a bowl. Add the coconut cream or milk, chia seeds, and stevia, and mix well. Transfer the mixture into small glasses and refrigerate for at least 2 hours before serving. (After 2 hours the chia seeds will have swollen and formed a gel with the coconut cream, creating a thick pudding with a slight crunch from the seeds.)

4. Divide the berries equally between the glasses and serve.

PERFECT PIKELETS

These are perfectly fluffy, bite-size nourishing snacks and ideal for parties, playdates, and your little one's lunch box.

SERVES 4

Prep time: 10 minutes   **Cook time:** 3–4 minutes
Allergens: egg (whole egg suitable for 12+ months only)

2 free-range, organic eggs
1 banana, coarsely chopped
½ teaspoon ground cinnamon
1 teaspoon chia seeds
1–2 tablespoons cold-pressed, virgin coconut oil

TO SERVE
Raspberry Chia Jam (page 246)
½ banana, sliced

1. Place the eggs, banana, cinnamon, and chia seeds in a blender and blend until smooth. Heat a teaspoon of the coconut oil in a frying pan over medium heat.

2. Ladle 1½ to 2 tablespoons of batter into the pan for each pikelet, spreading each one slightly with the back of a spoon until they're about 1½ inches (4 cm) in diameter. Cook for 2 minutes on one side, until the tops dry out slightly and the bottoms start to brown. Flip and cook the other side for 1 minute. You will need to do this in batches, using a little more of the coconut oil each time.

3. Serve warm with Raspberry Chia Jam (page 246), fresh banana and, of course, oodles of love.

Note:

• If your child has a sensitive tummy, be mindful that this recipe contains chia seeds.

COUGH DROP GUMMIES

Here we have created a sore throat treat with medicinal properties. These gummies have an amazing taste and texture that the whole family will love.

MAKES 40 GUMMIES

Prep time: 20 minutes (plus 15 minutes to set)   **Cook time:** 3 minutes   **Allergens:** none

1 cup (250 ml) boiling water
2 sticks lemongrass, smashed with the back of a knife to releases the juices before adding it to water
2-inch (5-cm) piece ginger, chopped
3½ tablespoons grass-fed gelatin
½ teaspoon ground turmeric
3 tablespoons lemon juice
2 tablespoons manuka honey or raw honey

1. Place the boiling water, lemongrass, ginger, and gelatin in a small bowl and stir until the gelatin powder dissolves. Allow to stand for 10 minutes so the lemongrass and ginger can infuse. Stir the turmeric, lemon juice, and honey into the liquid and mix until the honey has dissolved.

2. Pass the liquid through a fine strainer and discard the lemongrass and ginger, then pour the mixture into a silicone ice-cube tray or mini silicone molds, pouring in ⅓ ounce (10 ml) per cavity.

3. Place the trays/molds immediately in the freezer for approximately 15 minutes. Once the gummies have set, remove them from the tray and store in an airtight jar or container. They will keep for a few weeks in the fridge.

NUT-FREE BANANA BREAD

Banana bread has become a popular treat for many kids and adults. With this recipe, we have created a healthier option that is nut free, so it can be taken to school. Having said that, this still contains a high amount of natural sugars and should be viewed as a treat to enjoy in small quantities from time to time.

SERVES 6–8
MAKES 1 8-INCH (20-CM) LOAF

Prep time: 10 minutes   **Cook time:** 1 hour   **Allergens:** none

3 tablespoons coconut oil, melted, plus extra for greasing and serving

²⁄₃ cup (80 g) coconut flour

1 teaspoon baking soda

1 teaspoon ground cinnamon

Pinch sea salt

6 very ripe bananas

4 eggs

¼ teaspoon vanilla powder or 1 vanilla pod, split and seeds scraped

¼ cup (90 g) honey, plus extra for brushing

1 tablespoon apple cider vinegar

1. Preheat the oven to 350°F (180°C). Grease an 8 × 4-inch (20 × 10 cm) loaf pan with a little coconut oil, then line the base and sides with parchment paper.

2. In a large bowl, combine the coconut flour, baking soda, cinnamon, and salt and mix well. Place five bananas in a bowl and mash thoroughly. Slice the remaining banana diagonally into eight pieces. Set aside.

3. In another bowl, whisk together the eggs, vanilla, honey, and vinegar, then stir in the mashed banana.

4. Pour the liquid ingredients into the dry ingredients and stir with a wooden spoon until thoroughly combined. Add the coconut oil and continue stirring until incorporated.

5. Spoon the batter into the prepared loaf pan and spread out evenly with a spatula. Arrange the reserved banana slices on top and bake for 1 hour, or until a skewer inserted in the center comes out clean. Allow the bread to cool in the pan for 10 minutes, then carefully turn out onto a wire rack.

6. Brush a little extra honey over the top and allow to cool for 20 to 30 minutes. Slice and serve toasted, spread with some coconut oil.

NUT-FREE MUESLI BARS

MAKES ABOUT 10

Prep time: 20 minutes (plus 2–3 hours to set)   **Cook time:** n/a   **Allergens:** none

1 ripe banana, coarsely chopped
½ cup (120 ml) coconut oil, melted
⅔ cup (90 g) cacao butter, melted
⅓ cup (80 g) hulled tahini
¼ cup (100 g) honey or maple syrup
¼ teaspoon sea salt
1½ teaspoons ground cinnamon
¾ cup (100 g) pumpkin seeds
1 cup (125 g) sunflower seeds
2 tablespoons chia seeds
2 tablespoons flaxseeds
3 tablespoons sesame seeds, toasted
1 cup (60 g) shredded coconut
3 tablespoons currants

1. Line the base and sides of a 9½ × 7-inch (24 × 18 cm) baking pan with parchment paper.

2. Place the banana, coconut oil, cacao butter, tahini, honey or maple syrup, salt, and cinnamon in the bowl of a food processor and blend to a smooth, runny paste.

3. Place the seeds in a large bowl, then stir in the shredded coconut. Pour over the banana mixture and mix until well combined.

4. Spoon the seed mixture into the prepared pan and smooth using a palette knife or spatula, then evenly sprinkle the currants over the top. Cover and refrigerate for 2 to 3 hours until set. Cut into even-size bars and store in an airtight container in the fridge for up to 1 week.

CHOCOLATE-CHIP COOKIES

Who doesn't love a cookie? Especially when they are free of gluten and refined sugar. And to top it off, let's make them nut free so that kids can take them to school as a treat from time to time.

MAKES 12 COOKIES

Prep time: 20 minutes **Cook time:** 20–23 minutes **Allergens:** dairy (ghee, chocolate)

¾ cup (130 g) cassava flour
¼ cup (30 g) coconut flour
Pinch fine salt
1 teaspoon baking soda
¾ cup (185 ml) ghee, melted
¼ cup (60 ml) maple syrup
½ cup (80 g) coconut sugar
1 teaspoon vanilla extract
1 cup (110 g) chopped dark chocolate
    (70–90% cacao)

1. Preheat the oven to 320°F (160°C).

2. Line two large baking sheets with parchment paper. In a large bowl, combine the cassava and coconut flours, salt, and baking soda and mix well. Add the ghee, maple syrup, coconut sugar, vanilla, and chopped chocolate and mix to form a sticky dough.

3. Divide the dough evenly into 12 pieces, then roll into golf ball–size balls and place on the prepared sheets, allowing room for spreading. Gently press down on each dough ball with your hand. Bake for 20 to 23 minutes until golden. Cool on the baking sheet. Serve or store in an airtight container in the pantry for up to 5 days.

Note:

• Make sure the dark chocolate you use for this recipe is free of both sugar and dairy.

COCONUT JELLY WITH BERRIES

These will be sure-fire winners at your next birthday party and can be made a day or two beforehand. I've made these without added sweeteners, just the water from a young coconut, but you can add some honey or coconut nectar if you prefer. Your best bet is to use fresh young coconuts that you open yourself. You can use packaged coconut water but look for one without additives. If you are adventurous, you can also make savory versions of these jellies. Try using slow-cooked meat or cooked prawns with tarragon in a fish stock. You'll need six small bowls, cups, or jelly molds for this recipe.

SERVES 6

Prep time: 10–15 minutes (plus 4 hours to set)   **Cook time:** 3 minutes
Allergens: none

2 cups (500 ml) coconut water, *divided*
1 tablespoon powdered gelatin
Coconut nectar or honey, to taste,
    optional
1½ cups (240 g) mixed berries (such as
    raspberries, blueberries, strawberries,
    and blackberries), plus extra for
    serving
Flesh of 1 young coconut
    (about ½ cup/100 g), chopped
1 tablespoon chia seeds

1. Place 3 tablespoons of the coconut water in a small saucepan and sprinkle over the gelatin. Allow to soak for 2 minutes. Place the pan over medium heat and, stirring gently, bring to a simmer and heat until the gelatin has completely dissolved. Remove from the heat and set aside.

2. In a bowl, whisk the remaining coconut water with the coconut nectar or honey, if using. Stir in the gelatin mixture, then pour the jelly mixture into six 4¼-ounce (125 ml) cups or jelly molds until three-quarters full. Add some berries and coconut flesh and sprinkle on some chia seeds. Chill the jellies for 4 hours, or until set.

3. Remove the jellies from the molds by placing the molds in a bath of hot water for a few seconds (be careful not to submerge in the water), then turn out onto serving plates. Serve with a scattering of fresh berries.

FRUIT SALAD POPSICLES

I can still remember the instantly refreshing feeling you get from sucking on an ice-cold Popsicle on a hot summer's day, so I just had to include a recipe that you and your kids can easily make at home. They take no time at all to prepare, but they do take about 6 hours to freeze, so it's best to make them the night before, otherwise you'll have hungry munchkins hanging around the kitchen hankering for the pops to freeze. Some of my favorite fruits to use are antioxidant-rich berries, refreshing watermelon, and mangoes with a squeeze of lime juice.

SERVES 8

Prep time: 15–20 minutes   **Cook time:** n/a   **Allergens:** none

2 young coconuts
Selection of fruit of your choice (such as strawberries, grapes, mangoes, lychees, kiwi fruit, raspberries, pineapple)

1. Open the coconuts by cutting a circular hole in the top of each one. Strain the coconut water and set aside.

2. Cut the fruit into bite-size pieces (not too small—you want to enjoy the lovely texture of frozen fruit). Arrange the fruit in eight 2¾-ounce (80 ml) Popsicle molds, making sure the pieces fit very snugly. Pour enough coconut water into each mold to just cover the fruit.

3. Insert a Popsicle stick in the middle of each mold and freeze until solid, about 6 hours.

CAROB BARK

Carob powder is made from the pod of the carob tree and is a great substitute for cacao if you want to avoid caffeine. You can also add carob power or cacao to your smoothies, tea, coffee, or desserts. It's best to choose the raw organic options that are available.

YIELD: 1 (9 × 7¾ INCH/23 × 20 cm) SLAB

Prep time: 10 minutes (plus 20 minutes setting)
Cook time: 2 minutes   **Allergens:** nuts

1½ cups (220 g) cocoa butter
6 tablespoons carob powder, sifted
2 tablespoons cold-pressed, virgin coconut oil
2 tablespoons raw honey or green leaf stevia powder to taste, *optional*
¼ cup (30 g) goji berries
½ cup (50 g) walnuts, activated if possible (page 245)
½ cup (80 g) almonds, activated if possible (page 245)
¼ cup (30 g) pumpkin seeds
¼ teaspoon ground cinnamon

1. Melt the cocoa butter in a large bowl over a saucepan of simmering water (about a quarter full) and stir with a spatula until melted. Make sure no water gets into the cocoa butter and that the pan doesn't touch the water.

2. Remove from the heat and stir in the carob powder, coconut oil, and raw honey or stevia (if using). Make sure all the ingredients are well incorporated.

3. Add the goji berries, walnuts, almonds, pumpkin seeds, and cinnamon and mix thoroughly. Set aside.

4. Line a 9 × 7¾-inch (23 × 20 cm) pan with parchment paper. Pour the carob and nut mixture onto the lined pan and spread evenly with a palette knife or spatula.

5. Chill in the freezer for 20 minutes or until set. Peel off the parchment paper and cut or break the carob into pieces.

6. Store in an airtight container in the refrigerator for up to 2 weeks.

COCONUT CUPCAKES

These cupcakes are wonderfully nourishing, full of good fats and fiber—an ideal baked treat for parties!

MAKES 9 CUPCAKES

Prep time: 20 minutes (plus 8 hours chilling)
Cook time: 20–25 minutes (plus 20 minutes resting)   **Allergens:** egg

4 free-range, organic eggs
½ cup (125 ml) maple syrup or honey
⅓ cup (80 ml) cold-pressed, virgin coconut oil or ghee, melted
½ cup (70 g) coconut flour
1 teaspoon baking soda
2 teaspoons lemon juice
2 tablespoons coconut cream
1 teaspoon vanilla extract
Chia seeds, to decorate

WHIPPED COCONUT CREAM

1 (13½-oz/400-ml) can organic coconut cream
1 tablespoon maple syrup or raw honey

Notes:

- I do the mixing in my KitchenAid and it works a treat, though it would work just as well with a hand blender.

- If you use honey, it's best not to serve the cupcakes to babies until they're 12+ months.

1. To make the whipped coconut cream, place the unopened can of coconut cream in a stainless-steel mixing bowl and refrigerate overnight.

2. Open the can of chilled coconut cream and scoop out the hardened cream into the chilled bowl. (Store the coconut water in a sealed container in the fridge for another use—it's perfect to add to smoothies.)

3. Add the maple syrup or honey to the cream. Use an electric mixer to beat the hardened coconut cream and maple syrup or honey on high until soft peaks form (3 to 5 minutes). Allow the cream to set in the fridge for 40 minutes before serving.

4. Preheat the oven to 350°F (180°C). Line a 9-cup muffin pan with cupcake liners. Place the eggs, maple syrup or honey, and coconut oil or ghee in a bowl and mix well.

5. Gradually add the flour, baking soda, lemon juice, coconut cream, and vanilla, mixing well between each ingredient addition. Allow the batter to sit for a few minutes to thicken.

6. Spoon a few heaped tablespoons of batter into each cupcake liner, until each is three-quarters full. Bake for 20 to 25 minutes, or until a skewer inserted into the center of a cupcake comes out clean.

7. Remove the muffin pan from the oven and allow to sit for 20 minutes. Remove the cupcakes from the pan and allow to cool completely.

8. To serve, spread a spoonful of the coconut cream over the top of the cooled cupcakes using the back of a tablespoon or a small palette knife, then sprinkle with chia seeds.

CHINDII COOKIES

My wife Nicola came up with this recipe for our two daughters, Chilli and Indii, when they were quite young. They all got into the kitchen together to make some cookies that Nic created on the spot, and the girls loved them so much that Nic and the girls decided to come up with a name for them that is a combination or Chilli and Indii's first names . . . and the Chindii cookie was born.

MAKES 20 COOKIES

Prep time: 25 minutes **Cook time:** 40 minutes **Allergens:** sesame, nuts

3 tablespoons coconut flour
1 cup (90 g) dried coconut
1 cup (160 g) macadamia nuts
½ cup (40 g) quinoa flakes or coconut flakes
½ cup (60 g) sultanas or raisins (or any dried fruit), *optional*
2 teaspoons baking soda
Pinch Himalayan salt
1 cup (155 g) sesame seeds
½ cup (100 ml) coconut oil
½ cup (110 ml) maple syrup
4 tablespoons honey
1 teaspoon natural vanilla extract
2 eggs, lightly whisked

1. Preheat the oven to 275°F (140°C). Line a large baking sheet with parchment paper.

2. Combine the coconut flour, dried coconut, macadamias, quinoa or coconut flakes, sultanas or raisins, baking soda, and salt in a food processor and pulse a few times until a chunky paste forms. Transfer the coconut flour mixture into a bowl, mix in the sesame seeds, and set aside.

3. Melt the coconut oil in a saucepan over low heat, stir in the maple syrup, honey, and vanilla and bring to a simmer. Remove from the heat and set aside.

4. Add the eggs to the coconut flour mixture and stir to combine. Pour in the coconut oil mixture and stir well until you have a soft, sticky dough. Shape the dough into 20 walnut-size balls and use your hand to press them flat on the prepared baking sheet, allowing space for the cookies to spread. Bake for 30 to 40 minutes, or until golden. Transfer to a wire rack to cool before eating. Store in an airtight container for up to 1 week.

Tip:

- If the cookie dough seems too wet, just add some more dried coconut or some chia seeds; and if it's too dry, add some more coconut oil and a little water.

PART 4

DRINKS

It goes without saying that the purest, cleanest water, free of fluoride and chlorine and other toxic substances, is the optimal drink for human beings once they come off breast milk. Yet the choices these days for drinks and beverages are astounding. I have included a variety of recipes in the drinks section to add some variety and some different health options that fly in the face of many of the options available at convenience stores. I have focused on some real food ingredients to not only be delicious to our families' taste buds, but also be nutritionally beneficial for us too. There are some wonderful and satiating smoothies that the whole family will love, as well as some fermented drink recipes to add some healthy beneficial bacteria into our gut flora.

KETOGENIC CHOC–BERRY SMOOTHIE

A smoothie from time to time can bring a lot of joy to children (and parents too). The key, for me, is to make them so they are not loaded with sugars and carbohydrates, but instead some good-quality fat, so that they are not only delicious but satiating and filling. This recipe checks all of these boxes.

SERVES 2

Prep time: 5 minutes   **Cook time:** n/a   **Allergens:** none

1²/₃ cup (400 ml) coconut cream
½ cup (120 ml) coconut water
²/₃ cup (80 g) fresh or frozen mixed
  berries, plus extra to serve
6 mint leaves
1 egg
1 tablespoon sunflower seeds
1 tablespoon pumpkin seeds
1 tablespoon chia seeds
3 tablespoons cacao or carob powder
1 tablespoon grass-fed collagen powder

1. Place all the ingredients in a blender and blend until smooth. Serve in a tall milkshake glass or, if you're on the go, in a bottle. Finish with some extra berries, if you like.

Notes:

- If you prefer a little more sweetness, add stevia to taste.

- This smoothie can be made in advance, frozen and then popped in your lunch box to thaw. Just give it a good shake before drinking.

MACADAMIA AND BANANA SMOOTHIE

Macadamia nuts and bananas work really well together in a lot of different recipes, and here is a simple smoothie recipe that the whole family will love.

SERVES 1

Prep time: 5 minutes   **Cook time:** n/a   **Allergens:** none

1 large banana, frozen

¼ vanilla pod, split and seeds scraped, or a pinch of vanilla powder

Pinch ground cinnamon, plus extra to serve

5 macadamia nuts (activated if possible, see page 245)

¾ cup (185 ml) almond milk (to make your own, see page 243)

2 teaspoons flaxseed meal, *optional*

1 tablespoon honey or to taste, *optional*

1. Place all the ingredients in a blender and blend until smooth. Pour into a glass, dust with an extra pinch of cinnamon, and serve immediately.

EGGNOG

This nonalcoholic paleo version of the Christmas favorite provides a great protein hit and is delicious served chilled. I have suggested coconut milk, but you can use any type of nut milk. You could even freeze the eggnog in Popsicle molds if you want to create an icy Christmas treat.

SERVES 4

Prep time: 5 minutes   **Cook time:** 6–12 minutes   **Allergens:** none

4 egg yolks
2 tablespoons coconut sugar or maple syrup, or to taste
2 (13½-ounce/400-ml) cans coconut milk
½ teaspoon ground cinnamon, plus extra to serve
1 teaspoon freshly grated nutmeg, plus extra to serve
Almond milk (to make your own, see page 224), to serve

1. In the bowl of an electric mixer with a whisk attachment, whisk the egg yolks for a couple of minutes until doubled in size. Gradually add the coconut sugar or maple syrup and whisk for 1 minute. Set aside.

2. Combine the coconut milk, cinnamon, and nutmeg in a saucepan over medium heat and bring to a gentle simmer.

3. Turn the electric mixer to low and gradually whisk the hot spiced coconut milk into the egg yolk mixture until well combined.

4. Pour the mixture into a clean saucepan and stir gently but constantly over low heat for 5 to 10 minutes, or until the mixture thickens and coats the back of the spoon. Be patient with this process; if you turn the heat up too high or don't stir, the mixture might turn into scrambled eggs. Remove from the heat and mix in some rum, if you desire. Set the pan over a bowl of ice water to stop the cooking process, stirring occasionally for 2 minutes. (Be careful, you don't want water overflowing into the eggnog!). Cover with plastic wrap and place the fridge to chill. (The longer you let it chill, the thicker it will become.)

5. Before serving, add the desired amount of almond milk to thin the eggnog and sprinkle with some extra nutmeg and cinnamon.

KOMBUCHA

Kombucha is made by fermenting sweet tea. It helps with digestion and strengthens your immune system. The tea is cultured with a SCOBY, which is a colony of bacteria and yeasts. A SCOBY is usually created by feeding and growing these particular sets of bacteria; as they grow they are then divided and shared with others. If you don't know anyone who can give you a SCOBY, you can purchase them online or through specialist fermenters. You can also create your own SCOBY from a bottle of kombucha bought from a health food store. You can use black, green, oolong, or white tea as a base for your kombucha, and by adding sugar you create an energy source for the SCOBY. The sugar is eaten up by the bacteria, so there is very little left in the final product.

MAKES 1 GALLON

Prep time: 5–10 minutes (plus 2–3 weeks to ferment)   **Cook time:** n/a   **Allergens:** none

1 cup (250 g) organic raw sugar
5 teaspoons organic loose-leaf
   black tea
1 cup (250 ml) finished kombucha
Liquid (from a previous batch, a store-
   bought bottle, or from the liquid the
   SCOBY comes in)
1 kombucha SCOBY

1. Bring 3 cups (750 ml) of filtered water to a boil in a stainless-steel saucepan. Add the sugar or other sweetener and stir until dissolved.

2. Remove from the heat and add the loose-leaf tea. Allow to cool. Pour the sweet tea through a fine plastic strainer into a 3½-quart (3.5-L) glass jar with a wide mouth (don't use metal or plastic as these materials can damage the cultures in the SCOBY). Add the finished kombucha liquid and SCOBY to the jar, along with 2½ quarts (2.4 l) of filtered water.

3. Cover the top of your jar with cheesecloth and secure it with a rubber band. Leave undisturbed for 2 or 3 weeks in a warm, dark place—you are aiming for 64–82°F (18–28°C). On top of the fridge works well, or, if you live in a colder climate, you can use a heating mat like those used for seedlings. As your kombucha ferments, a new SCOBY will grow attached to the original one to the width of your container.

4. After a week of fermenting, taste your kombucha to determine if it's ready to drink. It should be moderately fizzy and have a sweet and sour flavor, with a slight hint of tea. If the mixture still tastes too sweet, leave it to ferment for a few

more days. If you're happy with the taste, use clean hands to remove the SCOBY and separate it from the new one. You will now have two SCOBYs, which you can use to make more kombucha (or you can give one to a friend who is interested in making their own).

5. If you don't want to make another batch of kombucha straight away, you can store the SCOBYs in a solution of sweetened tea on the counter. Don't put the SCOBYs in the fridge or they will go into hibernation.

6. Transfer the kombucha to sterilized glass bottles for storage, leaving about ⅔ inch (1½ cm) of headspace at the top. Allow the bottled kombucha to sit at room temperature for a day or two to ferment a bit more and to build up carbonation, then refrigerate until ready to drink. The kombucha will last in the fridge for up to 3 months, but it's better to drink it sooner rather than later.

Tips:

- You will need four 1-quart (1-L) sterilized glass bottles to store your finished kombucha. To sterilize the bottles, wash them in very hot, soapy water and run them through a hot rinse cycle in your dishwasher.

- If you don't have a dishwasher, boil the bottles in a large pot on the stove for 10 minutes, then place on a pan in a 300°F (150°C) oven for 10 minutes, or until dry.

BEET KVASS

We enjoy a nonalcoholic fermented beverage every single day upon waking or just before a meal. The types of drink that we make and consume always vary, as they all have their own special properties; favorites include nondairy kefir, kvass, or kombucha. When we have beets on hand and leftover kraut juice from the jar, we love to make kvass. It is so good for cultivating beneficial gut bacteria.

MAKES 6 CUPS (1.5 LITERS)

Prep time: 15 minutes   **Cook time:** n/a   **Allergens:** none

2–4 beets (about 1¼ lb/550 g)
1 tablespoon sea salt
1 cup (250 ml) filtered water, plus extra
½ sachet vegetable starter culture
   or 3 tablespoons sauerkraut brine
   (to make your own sauerkraut, see
   page 216)

1. You'll need a 1.5-quart (1.5-L) preserving jar with an airlock lid for this recipe. Wash the jar and all utensils in very hot water or run them through a hot rinse cycle in the dishwasher.

2. Wash and scrub the beets (peel them if they are not organic), then chop into ¾-inch (2-cm) cubes and place them in the jar.

3. Mix the salt, water, and starter culture or sauerkraut brine in a glass measuring jug, then pour into the jar.

4. Fill the jar with filtered water, leaving ¾ inch (2 cm) free at the top, and tightly secure the lid. Leave on the kitchen counter at room temperature for 4 to 7 days to ferment. Strain and chill before drinking.

5. The kvass will keep for 2 weeks in the fridge once opened.

Note:

- Your kvass may develop a thin layer of white or brown foam on top during the fermentation process. This is harmless—simply scoop it out with a spoon before placing the kvass in the fridge to chill.

YOUNG COCONUT KEFIR

Kefir is a great source of vitamins, minerals, probiotics, and a variety of other unique compounds that can greatly contribute to your and your kids' overall health and well-being. Kefir was traditionally made using raw milk that was then fermented; however, I much prefer using either coconut milk or coconut water. Try experimenting with different fruits and herbs for added flavor and medicinal qualities.

MAKES ABOUT 1½ QUARTS (1.5 L)

Prep time: 10 minutes   **Cook time:** n/a   **Allergens:** none

3–4 fresh young coconuts
1 packet vegetable starter culture (this will weigh ⅛ oz/5 g, depending on the brand)

1. You will need a 1½-quart (1.5-L) preserving jar or bottle with an airlock lid for this recipe. Wash the jar, a small saucepan, and a spoon in hot soapy water, then sterilize them by running them through a hot rinse cycle on your dishwasher.

2. Open the coconuts by cutting circular holes in the tops. Strain the coconut water into the sterilized saucepan, place over low heat, and bring to 88–90°F (31–32°C). Use a candy thermometer to check the temperature or wash your hands very well and dip in your finger. At 90°F (32°C), it will feel lukewarm, just below body temperature. Be careful not to heat it above 99°F (37°C), as the microflora and many of the enzymes and vitamins will be destroyed.

3. Pour the coconut water into the sterilized jar, then add the starter culture and stir with the sterilized spoon until dissolved. Close the lid and put in a dark place (a cooler is good) to ferment at 70–75°F (21–24°C) for 36 to 48 hours.

4. Your kefir is ready when the water turns from relatively clear to cloudy white. Taste test it after 36 hours by pouring some into a glass. It should taste tart and tangy, like champagne. If it still tastes sweet, leave it for a little longer. Once ready, it will last for up to 2 weeks in the fridge.

Variations:

STRAWBERRY AND MINT KEFIR

Wash and halve eight strawberries, then add them to the finished fermented kefir with a small handful of mint leaves. Close the lid, place in a dark spot, and leave to ferment at 70– 75°F (21–24°C) for a further 24 hours. Pour into a sterilized glass jug with a lid and refrigerate. Strain and discard the fruit pulp before drinking.

RASPBERRY, CLOVE, AND GINGER KEFIR

Add 2 ounces (60 g) of raspberries, 6 cloves, and 1 tablespoon finely grated ginger to the finished fermented kefir. Close the lid and place in a dark spot to ferment at 70–75°F (21–24°C) for a further 24 hours. Pour into a sterilized glass jug with a lid and refrigerate. Strain before drinking.

Tips:

- It is important that all materials that come into contact with the kefir are sterilized. You want to grow good bacteria, not the bad stuff, so boil or wash everything in very hot water. Also make sure you wash your hands well before starting.

- Glass jars and storage bottles are preferable to plastic since kefir actually breaks down plastic and you may end up eating it. Limited contact is fine, but prolonged contact is discouraged.

- It is very important that you use coconut water from fresh young coconuts. Store-bought varieties do not work as they are pasteurized.

PART 5
Fermented Foods

Human beings have been making fermented foods for millennia, perhaps by accident at first, through to the wide range of fermented foods and drinks that are available now in health food stores, supermarkets, and famers markets as well as people's home kitchens. These tried and tested recipes come from different cultures from around the world, and we love to include them in our lifestyle not only for the taste, but for the goodness that they can bring us.

KID-FRIENDLY KIMCHI

MAKES 1 × 1.5-QUART (1.5-L) JAR

Prep Time: 15 minutes (plus 10–14 days to ferment)
Cook time: n/a   **Allergens:** none

1 pound (450 g) red cabbage
1 pound (450 g) cabbage
¼ daikon (white radish), diced
1 green apple, cored and julienned
1 red onion, thinly sliced
1 French shallot, thinly sliced
1 handful cilantro leaves, chopped
Juice of 1 lemon
1½ teaspoons sea salt
1 sachet vegetable starter culture (⅛ oz/5 g, depending on the brand)

1. You will need a 1.5-quart (1.5-L) preserving jar with an airlock lid for this recipe. Wash the jar and all the utensils you will be using in very hot water. Dry well and set aside. Alternatively, run them through a hot rinse cycle in the dishwasher.

2. Remove the outer leaves of the cabbages. Choose an unblemished leaf, wash it well, and set aside for later. Shred the cabbages in a food processor or slice with a knife or mandolin, then transfer to a large glass or stainless-steel bowl. Add the daikon, apple, onion, shallot, cilantro, lemon juice, and salt and mix well. Cover and set aside.

3. Prepare the starter culture according to the directions on the packet. Add to the vegetables and mix thoroughly. Using a large spoon, fill the prepared jar with the vegetable mixture, pressing down to remove any air pockets and leaving ¾ inch (2 cm) of room at the top. The vegetables should be completely submerged in the liquid. Add more water if necessary.

4. Take the clean cabbage leaf, fold it up, and place it on top of the mixture, then add a small glass weight (a shot glass is ideal) to keep everything submerged. Close the lid, then wrap a dish towel around the side of the jar to block out the light.

5. Store the jar in a dark place with a temperature of 61–75°F (16–23°C) for 10–14 days. You can place the jar in a cooler to maintain a more consistent temperature. Different vegetables have different culturing times, and the warmer it is the shorter the time needed. The longer you leave it to ferment, the higher the level of good bacteria and the tangier the flavor.

6. Chill before eating. Once opened, the kimchi will last for up to 2 months in the fridge when kept submerged in liquid. If unopened, it will keep for up to 9 months in the fridge.

SAUERKRAUT

In my perfect world, people would give jars of homemade sauerkraut as a gift for birthdays, Christmas, and Valentine's Day instead of boxes of sugar-laden chocolates! Real fermented sauerkraut (not the stuff on the supermarket shelf that isn't refrigerated) is the simplest and most effective way to create good gut health. On top of that, fermented veggies are dirt cheap to make and absolutely delicious.

YIELD: 1½ QUARTS (1½ L)

Prep time: 15 minutes (plus 10–14 days fermenting)   **Cook time:** n/a   **Allergens:** none

1 star anise

1 teaspoon whole cloves

1½ pounds (650 g) cabbage (green or red, or a mix of the two)

1½ teaspoons sea salt

2 teaspoons caraway seeds

2 tablespoons juniper berries

1 small handful dill, coarsely chopped

1 sachet vegetable starter culture (⅛ oz/5 g, depending on the brand)

1. You will need a 1½-quart (1½-L) preserving jar with an airlock lid for this recipe. Wash the jar and utensils thoroughly in very hot water or run them through a hot rinse cycle in the dishwasher.

2. Place the star anise and cloves in a small piece of muslin, tie into a bundle, and set aside. Remove the outer leaves of the cabbage. Choose one of the outer leaves, wash it well, and set aside. Shred the cabbage in a food processor or slice by hand or with a mandolin, then place in a large glass or stainless-steel bowl.

3. Sprinkle the salt, caraway seeds, juniper berries, and dill over the cabbage. Mix well, cover, and set aside while you prepare the starter culture.

4. Dissolve the starter culture in water according to the packet instructions (the amount of water will depend on the brand you are using). Add to the cabbage with the muslin bag containing the spices and mix well.

5. Fill the prepared jar with the cabbage mix, pressing down firmly between each addition with a large spoon or potato masher to remove any air pockets. Leave ¾ inch (2 cm) of room free at the top. The cabbage should be completely submerged in the liquid, so add more water if necessary.

6. Take the clean cabbage leaf, fold it up, and place it on top of the mixture, then add a small glass weight to keep everything submerged (a small

shot glass is ideal). Close the lid, then wrap a dish towel around the side of the jar to block out the light. Store in a dark place with a temperature of 61–75°F (16–23°C) for at least 10 days and up to 2 weeks. (You can place the jar in a cooler to maintain a more consistent temperature.)

7. Different vegetables have different culturing times, and the warmer it is the shorter the time needed. The longer you leave the jar to ferment, the greater the level of good bacteria will be present. It's up to you how long you leave it—some people prefer the tangier flavor that comes with extra fermenting time, while others prefer a milder flavor.

8. Chill before eating. Once opened, it will last for up to 2 months in the fridge when kept submerged in the liquid. If unopened, it will keep for up to 9 months in the fridge.

Tips:

- A vegetable starter culture is a preparation used to kick-start the fermentation process when culturing vegetables. I prefer to use a broad-spectrum starter sourced from organic vegetables rather than one grown from dairy sources, as this ensures your fermented product will contain the highest number of living, active bacteria and will produce consistently successful results free of pathogens.

- Vegetable starter culture usually comes in sachets and can be purchased at health food stores or online.

BEGINNERS' KRAUT

Fermented vegetables will become a staple in homes over the next decade, not only because they taste amazing, but because of the scientific evidence coming out about how beneficial they are for our health. By including fermented vegetables in our diet, we are healing our second brain—our gut—and the truth of the matter is that many diseases originate in the gut, so the goal is to make the gut super healthy. One of the ways we can do this is by encouraging healthy bacteria. This child-friendly kraut is the perfect place to start—try adding half a teaspoon per meal and gradually build up to a tablespoon per meal and perhaps 2 tablespoons per meal for adults. It is super cheap to make, and you might even become addicted to it.

MAKES 1½ QUARTS (1½ L)

Prep time: 15 minutes (plus 10–14 days fermenting)   **Cook time:** n/a   **Allergens:** none

1 pound (450 g) green cabbage
1 pound (450 g) red cabbage
1 beet, peeled
2 carrots (about 8¾ oz/250 g in total)
1½ teaspoons sea salt
1 sachet vegetable starter culture (this
   will weigh ⅛ oz/5 g, depending on
   the brand)

1. You will need a 1.5-quart (1.5-L) preserving jar with an airlock lid for this recipe. Wash the jar and all the utensils you will be using in very hot water. Alternatively, run them through a hot rinse cycle in the dishwasher. Remove the outer leaves of the cabbages. Choose an unblemished leaf, wash it well, and set aside.

2. Shred the cabbages, beet, and carrots in a food processor or slice with a knife or mandolin, then transfer to a large glass or stainless-steel bowl.

3. Sprinkle the salt over the vegetables, mix well, and cover with a plate. Prepare the starter culture according to the directions on the packet. Add to the vegetables and mix thoroughly.

4. Using a large spoon, fill the prepared jar with the vegetable mixture, pressing down well to remove any air pockets and leaving 1 inch (2½ cm) free at the top. The vegetables should be completely submerged in the liquid. Add more water, if necessary.

5. Take the clean cabbage leaf, fold it up, and place it on top of the vegetables, then add a small glass weight (a shot glass is ideal) to keep everything submerged. Close the lid and wrap a dish towel

around the side of the jar to block out the light. Store in a dark place with a temperature of 61–75°F (16–23°C) for 10 to 14 days. (You can place the jar in a cooler to maintain a more consistent temperature.) Different vegetables have different culturing times, and the warmer it is the shorter the time needed. The longer you leave the jar, the higher the level of good bacteria present. It is up to you how long you leave it—some people prefer the tangier flavor that comes with extra fermenting time, while others prefer a milder flavor.

6. Chill before eating. Once opened, it will last for up to 2 months in the fridge when kept submerged in liquid. If unopened, it will keep for up to 9 months in the fridge.

PART VI

Breads, Wraps, and Crackers

A lot of us have grown up eating bread from a very young age, and for many it seems to be the hardest thing to give up when someone transitions to a grain-free diet. So, what are the options? Completely remove bread from the diet, which can have the possibility of upsetting family dynamics, or replace grain-filled breads for grain-free alternatives that can be less problematic for people's digestive systems and bodies? I personally love to still include grain- free bread options from time to time for myself and my family as they make a perfect vehicle for so many delicious offerings like pâté, avocado, sardines, eggs, and can also be used as croutons for soups, etc. I have included recipes for a variety of bread options, as well as wraps and crackers to play with for you and your family.

GLUTEN-FREE BREAD

This gluten-free "bread" is seriously satisfying, loaded with protein and fiber, and perfect for dipping into eggs or marrow. Keep some sliced in the freezer for toasting and serve with some beautiful Dairy-Free "Butter" (page 224).

SERVES 6–8 (MAKES 1 LOAF)

Prep time: 10 minutes   **Cook time:** 1 hour 20 minutes   **Allergens:** egg, nuts

1 cup (100 g) almond meal, sifted
½ cup (50 g) coconut flour, sifted
4 tablespoons psyllium seed powder
2 teaspoons gluten-free baking powder
8 free-range, organic eggs, beaten until fluffy
1 tablespoon apple cider vinegar
4 tablespoons cold-pressed, extra-virgin olive oil

1. Preheat the oven to 250°F/120°C. Grease a 7¾ × 4-inch (20 × 10 cm) loaf pan and line the base and sides with parchment paper.

2. Combine all of the dry ingredients in a large mixing bowl. Add the beaten eggs, apple cider vinegar, and olive oil, and stir well to combine.

3. Scoop the mixture into the loaf pan and spread out evenly to all four corners. Bake for 80 minutes or until a skewer inserted into the center comes out clean. Turn out onto a wire rack. Allow to cool a little, slice, then serve with whatever tickles your fancy. We love it dipped in olive oil, coconut aminos, and homemade dukkah.

Tip:

- Add a couple pinches of salt to the bread batter, if desired. It's recommended not to add salt to food for babies under 12 months. After 1 year, you can include a small amount of salt in your child's diet.

DAIRY-FREE "BUTTER"

We have come up with a delicious butter alternative and I think it's a real winner. It's delicious on our Gluten-Free Bread (page 223) or spooned onto your favorite steamed veggies . . . or just eat it by the spoonful.

MAKES 1 CUP (240 G)

Prep time: 5 minutes (plus 4 hours setting)   **Cook time:** n/a   **Allergens:** nuts

2 tablespoons organic coconut cream

4 tablespoons cold-pressed, virgin coconut oil, melted

6 tablespoons cold-pressed, extra-virgin olive oil or macadamia oil

1. Place all the ingredients in a food processor and blend until creamy. Pour into a small container or glass dish with a lid and refrigerate for 4 hours or until set.

2. Store in the refrigerator until needed.

Tip:

*   Add a couple pinches of salt to the butter mixture, if desired. It's recommended not to add salt to food for babies under 12 months. After 1 year, you can include a small amount of salt in your child's diet.

PALEO WRAPS

These wraps are so simple to make and will soon become a family favorite. Use them to whip up super-easy lunches for your household.

MAKES 7

Prep time: 10 minutes   **Cook time:** 20 minutes   **Allergens:** egg, sesame

4 eggs
2 tablespoons (20 g) sesame seeds, ground into a fine powder (use a spice grinder or mortar and pestle)
1 ounce (30 g) hemp seeds, ground into a fine powder (use a spice grinder or mortar and pestle)
½ teaspoon sea salt
½ teaspoon garlic powder
½ cup (60 g) tapioca flour
2½ tablespoons coconut oil or good-quality animal fat

1. Whisk the eggs, 2 tablespoons of water, the ground sesame and hemp seeds, and the salt, garlic powder, and tapioca flour together in a large bowl.

2. Melt 1 teaspoon of oil or fat in a 8-inch (20 cm) frying pan over medium heat and swirl around to coat the base of the pan.

3. Pour in about ¼ cup (60 ml) of batter and tilt and swirl the pan to spread the batter into a thin round. Cook for about 1 to 1½ minutes until lightly golden brown on the underside. Flip and cook on the other side for 30 seconds, or until lightly golden. Set aside on a plate.

4. Repeat with the remaining oil or fat and batter.

SUNFLOWER SEED CRACKERS

You are going to love making these crackers, as they are just so easy. They make the perfect light lunch or snack topped with your favorite dip or pâté.

MAKES 20 CRACKERS

Prep time: 25–35 minutes (plus 10 minutes resting time)
Cook time: 18–20 minutes   **Allergens:** none

4½ ounces (130 g) sunflower seeds
2½ ounces (70 g) tapioca flour, plus extra for dusting
2 tablespoons white or black chia seeds
½ teaspoon fine sea salt
¼ teaspoon baking powder
2 tablespoons filtered water
2 tablespoons apple cider vinegar
Extra-virgin olive oil, for brushing
Flaky sea salt, for sprinkling

1. Preheat the oven to 350°F (180°C).

2. Combine the sunflower seeds, tapioca flour, chia seeds, fine sea salt, and baking powder in the bowl of a high-speed blender or food processor and process to a fine powder.

3. Add the water and vinegar and continue to process until the dough comes together to form a sticky paste.

4. Transfer the dough to a work surface dusted with tapioca flour. Roll into a ball, place on a large sheet of parchment paper, and press down to flatten into a disc. Allow to rest for 10 minutes. Place another large sheet of parchment paper over the flattened dough and, using a rolling pin, roll out to a thickness of ⅛ inch (2 mm). Peel away the top sheet of paper and discard.

5. Using a pizza cutter or sharp knife, cut the dough into 2 × 3 inch (5 × 8 cm) rectangles. Transfer the dough shapes and the parchment paper to a baking sheet. Brush the shapes with a light coating of olive oil and sprinkle with the flaky salt. Bake, turning the baking sheet halfway through, for 18 to 20 minutes until golden.

6. Allow to cool completely before removing from the baking sheet and serving. The crackers can be stored in an airtight container in the pantry for up to 1 week.

NUT-FREE PALEO BREAD

ROUND ROLLS

MAKES 6

Prep time: 25–35 minutes   **Cook time:** 1½ hours   **Allergens:** egg

1 cup (70 g) psyllium husks

½ cup (70 g) coconut flour, plus extra for dusting

3 tablespoons chia seeds

3 tablespoons flaxseeds

¼ cup (30 g) pumpkin seeds, plus ¾ cup (80 g) extra, for sprinkling, *optional*

3 tablespoons sesame seeds

¼ cup (30 g) sunflower seeds

1 tablespoon coconut sugar or honey

2½ teaspoons baking powder

1½ teaspoons sea salt

1 tablespoon apple cider vinegar

2 cups (440 ml) water

3 eggs

2 tablespoons coconut oil, melted

1. Preheat the oven to 350°F (180°C).

2. Line a baking sheet with parchment paper. Place the psyllium husks, coconut flour, chia seeds, flaxseeds, pumpkin seeds, sesame seeds, and sunflower seeds in the bowl of a food processor and process for a few seconds until the seeds are finely chopped.

3. Transfer the flour mixture to a large bowl, then mix in the coconut sugar or honey, the baking powder, and the salt.

4. In another bowl, combine the vinegar, 2 cups (440 ml) of water, and the eggs and whisk until smooth. Add the coconut oil and the egg mixture to the dry ingredients and mix well to form a wet dough. Allow to stand for 2 minutes.

5. Knead the dough on a lightly floured work surface for 1 minute. Divide the dough into six portions and roll into balls. Place the dough balls on the prepared baking sheet, allowing room for spreading. Sprinkle with the extra pumpkin seeds if you like. Bake in the oven for 1 hour, rotating the baking sheet halfway through so the rolls cook evenly. To check if they are cooked, tap the base of a roll. If it sounds hollow, the rolls are ready. If they seem to be very heavy and dense, they need to cook for a little longer.

LONGROLLS

MAKES 6

1. Follow the steps above for preparing and kneading the dough. Divide the dough into six portions and roll into 4-inch-long (10-cm) log shapes. Place on the prepared baking sheet, allowing room for spreading, and bake in the oven for 1 hour, rotating the baking sheet halfway through so the rolls cook evenly. To check if they are cooked, tap the base of a roll. If it sounds hollow, the rolls are ready. If they seem to be very heavy and dense, they need to cook for a little longer. Dust with a little coconut flour, if desired.

BAGUETTE

MAKES 2

1. Follow the steps on the previous page for preparing and kneading the dough. Divide the dough into two portions and roll into 12-inch-long (30½-cm-long) log shapes. Place the dough portions on the prepared baking sheet, allowing room for spreading.

2. Cut four or five ⅓-inch-deep (1-cm-deep) diagonal slits across the top of each baguette. This is mainly decorative, so if you like you can skip this step. Bake in the oven for 1 hour, rotating the baking sheet halfway through so the baguettes cook evenly.

3. To check if they are cooked, tap the base of a baguette. If it sounds hollow, they are ready. If they seem to be very heavy and dense, cook for a little longer.

LOAF

MAKES 1 LOAF (10–12 SLICES)

1. Grease an 8 × 4-inch (20 × 10 cm) loaf pan and line the base and sides with parchment paper.

2. Follow the steps on the previous page for preparing and kneading the dough, then roll the dough into one big ball. Place the dough in the prepared loaf pan and pat down. Bake in the oven for 1½ hours, rotating the pan halfway through so the loaf cooks evenly. To check if it is cooked, turn out the loaf and tap the base. If it sounds hollow, it's ready. If the loaf seems to be very heavy and dense, return to the pan and cook for a little longer.

MACADAMIA FAT BOMB BREAD

Sara Karan, a cancer survivor who is featured in my documentary *The Magic Pill*, has kindly agreed to share her much-requested recipe for macadamia fat bomb bread—and here it is in all its glory. Thanks, Sarah!

MAKES 1 × 8-INCH (20-CM) LOAF (10–12 SLICES)

Prep time: 10 minutes   **Cook time:** 1 hour   **Allergens:** egg, nuts

1½ cups (225 g) macadamia nuts (activated if possible)
½ cup plus 1 tablespoon (140 g) almond butter (or other nut butter)
⅓ cup (80 ml) melted coconut oil
½ teaspoon fine sea salt
2 tablespoons apple cider vinegar
6 eggs
2 teaspoons baking powder

TO SERVE
Extra-virgin olive oil
Balsamic vinegar
Dukkah

1. Preheat the oven to 350°F (180°C). Grease an 8 × 4-inch (20 × 10 cm) loaf pan and line the base and sides with parchment paper, cutting into the corners to fit.

2. Blitz the macadamia nuts in a high-speed blender or food processor for about 6 minutes, or until a paste forms. Add the almond butter, coconut oil, salt, and vinegar and blend, scraping down the side from time to time, to a wet paste. Add the eggs and baking powder and blend to combine.

3. Scoop the mixture into the prepared pan and spread out evenly. Bake for 1 hour, rotating the pan halfway through so the loaf cooks evenly. To check if the bread is cooked, insert a skewer in the center; if it comes out clean, it's ready. Allow to cool a little in the tin, then turn out onto a wire rack to cool completely.

4. Thinly slice the bread and eat with whatever tickles your fancy. We love to dip this bread in olive oil, balsamic vinegar and homemade dukkah.

5. Store the bread in an airtight container in the fridge for up to 5 days or sliced in the freezer for up to 3 months.

CAULIFLOWER ROLLS

Serve these buns with your favorite fillings, such as ham, sliced tomato, fresh basil, and homemade mayonnaise.

MAKES 10 ROLLS

Prep time: 25 minutes   **Cook time:** 1 hour   **Allergens:** egg, sesame seeds

1¾ pounds (800 g) cauliflower florets

3 tablespoons tapioca flour, plus extra for dusting

¼ cup (35 g) coconut flour

2 teaspoons baking powder

½ teaspoon garlic powder

1¼ teaspoons fine sea salt

3 eggs, beaten

1 teaspoon apple cider vinegar

1 tablespoon sesame seeds

1 tablespoon poppy seeds

1. Preheat the oven to 350°F (180°C).

2. Line a baking sheet with parchment paper.

3. Place the cauliflower in the bowl of a food processor and process to very fine grains. Combine the flours, baking powder, garlic powder, and salt in a bowl and mix well. Add the cauliflower rice, eggs, and vinegar, then, using your hands, knead until the mixture comes together to form a ball. The dough will be wet and sticky.

4. Divide the dough into ten portions and shape them into rough balls with your hands. Place the dough balls on the prepared sheet, allowing room for spreading. Sprinkle on the sesame seeds and poppy seeds and bake for 1 hour, or until golden and a skewer inserted in the center of a roll comes out clean. (You need to do the skewer test as these rolls are more dense than regular bread rolls and won't sound hollow when you tap them.)

5. Transfer the rolls to a wire rack to cool.

6. Store the rolls in the fridge for up to 5 days or in the freezer for up to 3 months.

PART VII

Extras

A well-stocked pantry or refrigerator is one of life's luxuries and never to be underestimated, not just because of how much time this saves in the kitchen, but more important, just how much more delicious meal times become. Here are some terrific "extras" to have on hand.

MAYONNAISE

MAKES ABOUT 2 CUPS (500 ML)

Prep time: 10 minutes   **Cook time:** n/a   **Allergens:** none

4 egg yolks
2 teaspoons Dijon mustard
1 tablespoon apple cider vinegar
1 tablespoon lemon juice
1²/₃ cups (400 ml) olive oil
Sea salt and freshly ground black
  pepper

1. Place the egg yolks, mustard, vinegar, lemon juice, oil, and a pinch of salt in a glass jug or jar and blend with a handheld blender until smooth and creamy, working the blade from the bottom of the jug very slowly up to the top. Season with salt and pepper.

2. Alternatively, place the egg yolks, mustard, vinegar, lemon juice, and a pinch of salt in the bowl of a food processor and process until combined. With the motor running, slowly pour in the oil in a thin stream and process until thick and creamy. Season. Store in a sealed glass jar in the fridge for 4 or 5 days.

AÏOLI

MAKES 2 CUPS

Prep time: 5 minutes **Cook time:** n/a **Allergens:** none

6 roasted garlic cloves

4 egg yolks

2 teaspoons dijon mustard

2 teaspoons apple cider vinegar

1½ tablespoons lemon juice

1²/₃ cups olive oil

Sea salt and freshly ground black
  pepper

1. Place the garlic, egg yolks, mustard, vinegar and lemon juice in a food processor and blitz until combined.

2. With the motor running, slowly pour in the olive oil in a thin stream and process until the aïoli is thick and creamy. Alternatively, place all the ingredients except the salt and pepper in a glass jug and blend with a hand-held blender until smooth and creamy. Season with salt and pepper. Store in an airtight container in the fridge for up to 5 days.

GREEN GODDESS DRESSING

This versatile dressing can be whipped up in no time and keeps well in the fridge. Serve with veggies, patties, meatballs, or even zoodles (see Zoodle Bolognese, page 70). Leave out the anchovies for babies under 12 months.

MAKES 1 CUP (250 ML)

Prep time: 10 minutes   **Cook time:** n/a   **Allergens:** fish

½ avocado
3 tablespoons coconut milk
3 tablespoons lemon juice
1 clove garlic, finely chopped
2 anchovy fillets, finely chopped
½ cup (15 g) coarsely chopped parsley
3 tablespoons coarsely chopped basil leaves
1 tablespoon coarsely chopped tarragon leaves
½ cup (125 ml) cold-pressed, extra-virgin olive oil

1. Place all the ingredients except the olive oil in a food processor or blender and process until well combined.

2. With the motor running, slowly pour in the oil in a thin stream and process until the dressing thickens and the herbs are finely chopped.

3. Store in the refrigerator in a resealable glass jar for up to 5 days.

TOMATO KETCHUP

MAKES 1⅓ CUPS (330 G)

Prep time: 10 minutes   **Cook time:** 3 minutes   **Allergens:** none

¾ cup (185 g) tomato paste
½ cup (120 ml) filtered water
2 tablespoons apple cider vinegar
1 teaspoon garlic powder
1 teaspoon onion powder
½ teaspoon ground cinnamon
¼ teaspoon freshly grated nutmeg
2 teaspoons honey
Pinch ground cloves

1. Mix the tomato paste and water in a small saucepan. Place over medium heat and bring to a simmer (add more water if you prefer your ketchup to be thinner). Remove from heat and stir in the remaining ingredients until incorporated and smooth. Cool and store in an airtight glass jar in the fridge for up to 4 weeks.

CASHEW CHEESE

MAKES 1¼ CUPS

Prep time: 5 minutes, (plus 1–4 hours soaking)   **Cook time:** n/a   **Allergens:** nuts

1 cup (155 g) cashew nuts
2 teaspoons lemon juice
½ teaspoon sea salt
Pinch freshly ground black pepper
3 tablespoons filtered water

1. Soak the cashews in 3 cups of filtered water for 1 to 4 hours. Drain and rinse well.

2. Place the cashews in the bowl of a food processor, add the lemon juice, salt, and pepper and pulse for a minute to combine.

3. Add 3 tablespoons of filtered water and continue to process until smooth.

4. Store in an airtight glass container in the fridge for 5 to 7 days.

NUT MILK

Prep time: 8 minutes (plus 8–12 hours soaking)   **Cook time:** n/a   **Allergens:** nuts

1 cup (155 g) activated almonds or other nuts such as macadamia nuts or walnuts, soaked in filtered water overnight or at least 8 hours
1 liter filtered water

1. Drain the soaking nuts and rinse well. Place the nuts in a blender with the water and blend for a few minutes, or until smooth.

2. Line a bowl with a piece of muslin/cheesecloth so that the cloth hangs over the edges of the bowl (alternatively you can use a nut milk bag). Pour the blended nut and water mixture into the bowl. Pick up the edges of the cloth and squeeze out all the milk.

3. Pour the nut milk into a 1-quart (1-L) jar or bottle, then place it in the fridge to chill. Shake the bottle/jar before use as the milk will settle and separate after time. The nut milk will keep for 3 or 4 days refrigerated.

GARLIC CONFIT

MAKES 25 CLOVES

Prep time: 5–10 minutes   **Cook time:** 1 hour   **Allergens:** none

25 cloves garlic (about 100 g), peeled
1 cup (250 ml) melted coconut oil

1. Place the garlic and coconut oil in a saucepan over very low heat (do not allow the oil to boil).

2. Gently poach for 1 hour, or until the garlic is beautifully soft.

3. Transfer the garlic and oil to a sterilized glass jar, seal, and store in the fridge for up to 3 months.

ACTIVATED NUTS AND SEEDS

MAKES 3 CUPS

Prep time: 5 minutes (plus soaking time) **Cook time:** 6–24 hours **Allergens:** nuts

3 cups whole, raw nuts or seeds

1. Place the nuts/seeds in a bowl. Add enough filtered water to cover, then set aside to soak for the recommended soaking time:
   - Almonds: 12 hours
   - Brazil nuts: 12 hours
   - Cashews: 2–4 hours
   - Hazelnuts: 12 hours
   - Macadamia nuts: 7–12 hours
   - Pecans: 4–6 hours
   - Pistachio nuts: 4–6 hours
   - Pumpkin seeds: 7–10 hours
   - Sunflower seeds: 2 hours
   - Walnuts: 4–8 hours

2. After soaking, the nuts or seeds will look swollen and puffy and may even start to show signs of sprouting. Drain the water and rinse the nuts or seeds under running water.

3. In order to toast the nuts or seeds without damaging all the nutrients you've activated through soaking; you'll need to do so over low heat—either in a dehydrator or on the lowest temperature in your oven (at 120°F/50°C). This will take anywhere from 6 to 24 hours. The nuts or seeds are ready when they feel and taste completely dry.

4. Use your activated dried nuts or seeds as you normally would use toasted nuts or seeds. They keep well in an airtight container at room temperature and can also be ground into a flour for baking.

RASPBERRY CHIA JAM

MAKES 1 CUP (310 G)

Prep time: 5 minutes (plus 6 hours setting time)   **Cook time:** n/a   **Allergens:** none

3 tablespoons chia seeds

2 cups (250 g) frozen organic
   raspberries, thawed

2 tablespoons pure maple syrup, honey,
   or a few pinches of stevia (add more
   to taste if desired)

1. Place all the ingredients in a medium bowl. Stir to mix, making sure all the chia seeds have been moistened with the juice from the berries. Place in a food processor and pulse 2 or 3 times to break up the berries.

2. Pour the mixture into a glass jar or container, cover, and allow jam to thicken in the refrigerator for at least 6 hours. The jam will keep for 2 or 3 weeks in the refrigerator.

Thank You

A mountain of gratitude to my glorious family, especially my wonderful wife, Nic, and my two amazing daughters, Indii and Chilli. You three angels are a constant source of pure inspiration and happiness, and it is a humbling honor to walk beside you all throughout this life. Thank you for being your bright, fun-loving, authentic and unconditionally loving selves.

To the absolute wonder twins, Monica and Jacinta Cannataci, you both add your own magical essence to everything we create together, and this book just wouldn't be the same without your input. Thank you both for working so graciously and tirelessly, and for all that you do!

To the incredible photographers and food stylists I have worked with over the years. You all bring a unique sense of beauty that never ceases to be exceptionally pleasing, and I'm endlessly thankful to you all.

To Daniela Rapp, thank you so much for helping get this book to where it is now. So many people will benefit greatly from your skills and contributions.

To Robert (Bobby) Kennedy Jr., when you welcomed me into your home many years ago to create this relationship, I knew that this would be a wonderful journey together. I am pleased to call you my friend and mentor.

To all the team at Children's Health Defense, your determination, passion, and unwavering commitment to enriching children's and families' health is the benchmark for how to stand with integrity, authenticity, and love.

To Tony Lyons and Zoey O'Toole, thank you for the trust and support and encouragement to make this book available to all who need it.

A very warm thank you to my sweet mum, Joy. Among many things, you passed on your love of cooking and there's no doubt that I wouldn't be where I am without you.

I also wish to express a huge thank you to my teachers, peers, mentors, and friends, who are all genuinely working towards creating a healthier world and who are all in their own right true forces for good. A special mention goes out to the following friends who have helped me on this discovery of health over the years: Helen Padarin, Charlotte Carr, Rudy Eckhardt, Peter Bablis, Nora Gedgaudas, Dr. Kelly Brogan, Dr. William Davis, Dr. Natasha McBride, Professor Timothy Noakes, and many more.

Cheers,
Pete
www.peteevanschef.com
Cook with Love and Laughter!

Metric Conversions

If you're accustomed to using metric measurements, use these handy charts to convert the imperial measurements used in this book.

Weight (Dry Ingredients)

1 oz		30 g
4 oz	¼ lb	120 g
8 oz	½ lb	240 g
12 oz	¾ lb	360 g
16 oz	1 lb	480 g
32 oz	2 lb	960 g

Oven Temperatures

Fahrenheit	Celsius	Gas Mark
225°	110°	¼
250°	120°	½
275°	140°	1
300°	150°	2
325°	160°	3
350°	180°	4
375°	190°	5
400°	200°	6
425°	220°	7
450°	230°	8

Volume (Liquid Ingredients)

½ tsp.		2 ml
1 tsp.		5 ml
1 Tbsp.	½ fl oz	15 ml
2 Tbsp.	1 fl oz	30 ml
¼ cup	2 fl oz	60 ml
⅓ cup	3 fl oz	80 ml
½ cup	4 fl oz	120 ml
⅔ cup	5 fl oz	160 ml
¾ cup	6 fl oz	180 ml
1 cup	8 fl oz	240 ml
1 pt	16 fl oz	480 ml
1 qt	32 fl oz	960 ml

Length

¼ in	6 mm
½ in	13 mm
¾ in	19 mm
1 in	25 mm
6 in	15 cm
12 in	30 cm

Index